HARRAP'S ENGLISH CLASSICS

TEN TWENTIETH-CENTURY POETS

00612

G000269015

Ten Twentieth-century
Poets

EDITED WITH NOTES BY
MAURICE WOLLMAN M.A.

Nelson

Thomas Nelson and Sons Ltd
Nelson House   Mayfield Road
Walton-on-Thames   Surrey
KT12 5PL   UK

51 York Place
Edinburgh
EH1 3JD   UK

Thomas Nelson (Hong Kong) Ltd
Toppan Building 10/F
22A Westlands Road
Quarry Bay   Hong Kong

Thomas Nelson Australia
102 Dodds Street
South Melbourne
Victoria 3205   Australia

Nelson Canada
1120 Birchmount Road
Scarborough   Ontario
M1K 5G4   Canada

First published by Harrap Limited 1957
(under ISBN 0-245-52925-X)

Twenty-second impression published by Thomas Nelson and Sons Ltd 1987

ISBN 0-17-444163-0
NPN 9 8 7 6 5 4 3

Printed in Hong Kong.

PREFACE

THE introduction to each section of the anthology attempts to give a general view of the poet's work, but with special relevance to the selection that follows. The ideas put forward in these introductions and in the notes are condensed and are intended as sign-posts for the teacher to follow, commenting and adding as he goes, rather than dogmatic assertions for the student to learn and accept without question. Most of the ideas are capable of expansion and of illustration from the poems that follow.

ACKNOWLEDGMENTS

THANKS are due to the following for kind permission to print the poems included in this anthology:

W. H. Auden and Messrs Faber and Faber, Ltd, for poems from *Collected Shorter Poems 1930-44* and *The Shield of Achilles*; John Betjeman and Messrs John Murray, for poems from *Selected Poems* and *A Few Late Chrysanthemums*; the Executors of the late Walter de la Mare and Messrs Faber and Faber, Ltd, for poems from *Collected Poems*, *The Burning-glass*, *Inward Companion*, and *O Lovely England*; T. S. Eliot and Messrs Faber and Faber, Ltd, for poems from *Collected Poems 1909-35*; Robert Frost and Messrs Jonathan Cape, Ltd, for poems from *Collected Poems*; the Trustees of the Hardy Estate and Messrs Macmillan and Co., Ltd, for poems from *Collected Poems*, by Thomas Hardy; Edwin Muir and Messrs Faber and Faber, Ltd, for poems from *Collected Poems* and *One Foot in Eden*; Mrs Edward Thomas and Messrs Faber and Faber, Ltd, for poems from *Collected Poems*, by Edward Thomas; Mrs W. B. Yeats and Messrs A. P. Watt and Son, for poems from *Collected Poems of W. B. Yeats* (Macmillan); Andrew Young and Messrs Jonathan Cape, Ltd, for poems from *Collected Poems*.

INDEX OF AUTHORS

W. H. AUDEN (1907–73)

Born at York. Educated Gresham's School, Holt, and Christ Church, Oxford. After leaving the University he went to Berlin. On his return he became a schoolmaster before spending some time in documentary films—the verse commentary to *Night Mail* was composed by him. He drove an ambulance and served as stretcher-bearer on the Republican side during the Spanish Civil War. He travelled widely in Europe, as well as making visits to Iceland and China. In 1937 he was awarded the King's Medal for Poetry, and in 1945 he received the award of the American Academy of Art and Letters. In 1938 he went to the U.S.A., where he took up residence, lecturing at various schools and universities and becoming a naturalized American citizen. He returned to England as Professor of Poetry at Oxford 1956–61 (in succession to C. Day Lewis). Works include: *Poems* (1930); *The Orators* (1932); *The Dog beneath the Skin* (1935); *The Ascent of F6* (1936), and *On the Frontier* (1938)—with Christopher Isherwood—plays; *Look, Stranger!* (1936); *Letters from Iceland* (1937)—with Louis MacNeice; *Another Time* (1940); *New Year Letter* (1941); *For the Time Being* (1945); *The Age of Anxiety* (1948); *Collected Shorter Poems, 1930–1944* (1950); *Nones* (1952); *The Shield of Achilles* (1955).

W. H. Auden is primarily a poet of the 1930's. It was a time of uneasiness or, as he called it, an Age of Anxiety. Hanging above was the threat of war, which might lead to the end of civilization and the beginning of a new Dark Age. The rise to power of Mussolini and Fascism, and of Hitler and Nazism, was a constant and increasing menace of war and of the collapse of society. What was to be done to avert the peril was the question perpetually in the mind of thinking people. Some, among them poets and novelists, saw Communism as the possible answer; the Spanish Civil War of 1936 strengthened some in this belief and disabused others.

The growing belief in the theories of the subconscious, formulated by Adler, Jung, and Freud, took hold of men's minds and was reflected in literature. The terms of psychology crept more and more into poetry. The power of psycho-analysis to reveal the innermost secrets and workings of the human mind was accepted, and the more deeply the mind of man was revealed the less attractive was it.

In addition, the destruction and desolation that industrial development was bringing to the countryside was nearing its peak. The ugly signs of industrialization were more and more prominent—the slag heap, the derelict factory, the silted harbour, the opencast mining, the polluted river. Where was man to find peace and content in this modern world of imminent war, clashing ideologies, subconscious dark urgings, and ravished countryside? The answer given by some poets, including Auden, was "We must love another or die." Love, comradeship, community, are man's compensations.

In this century science and reason are playing a more and more important part in man's life. The imagination is being neglected, and experiences that only the imagination can apprehend are no longer valued. Auden speaks for the imagination, as did D. H. Lawrence.

Society is sick and ailing. Auden analyses clinically its symptoms, diagnoses its condition, and occasionally suggests a remedy. "The world is too much with us." Man is too preoccupied with the present, the materialistic, the transient. Auden feels that the crisis is urgent, that the individual must take his own share of responsibility, must try to improve society. He agrees with Wilfred Owen that "All the poet can do is to warn."

These are the themes of much of the poetry of the 30's, of the poems of, among others, Auden, Day Lewis, Spender, and MacNeice. Auden analyses the culture and society in which he lives. He expresses the common opinion on these aspects of modern life and he offers the common solution when he offers one. Sometimes the mood is satiric or ironic; often when it is ostensibly serious the ironic note creeps in. How else can one, in the face of inevitable disaster, show courage but by a smile or a jest that minimizes the disaster? Even love, the only answer that has validity, must not be taken too seriously, for if it fails there is nothing left, not even the jest. It follows, then, that Auden's main achievement is in the lyrical and the satirical.

Contemporary problems are seen with the eye of a competent reporter and expressed in contemporary language—colloquial, economical, concrete, spare, with the rhythms of everyday speech and idiom. The adjectives comment but do not describe. Detail is familiar and everyday. Similes surprise and are concise; the abstract is mated with the concrete. The metaphors and images are derived from modern life—climate, environment, industry, transport, urban pursuits, the sights and sounds of work and recreation. The language is sometimes obscure because of omissions or ellipses, its lack of sequence or its private metaphor, the difficult allusion or the technical terms of psychology; sometimes articles or relative pronouns or connectives are omitted.

Auden's moods are many; his sympathies and interests and curiosity are wide. He is observant, inventive and witty, and he writes with gusto and fluency. At times he shows the influence of Anglo-Saxon alliterative verse and of its later exponent, Langland, who taught him to use irony to comment on public and private life. He comes at other times under the influence of the facetious, exuberant Byron, or Yeats, or Housman, or Eliot, who showed him how to use irony to deal with modern urban life, or Hardy, with whom he shares an interest in the little gesture or movement that tells so much and is so revealing and significant and symbolic.

Many of his poems are new discoveries about the world we live in, showing us something that has always been there but that we have not had the eyes to see before. They show the meaning of experiences we have all undergone and the significance of the behaviour of individuals, classes, and nations.

Musée des Beaux Arts

About suffering they were never wrong,
The Old Masters: how well they understood
Its human position; how it takes place
While someone else is eating or opening a window or
        just walking dully along;
How, when the aged are reverently, passionately
        waiting
For the miraculous birth, there always must be
Children who did not specially want it to happen,
        skating
On a pond at the edge of the wood:
They never forgot
That even the dreadful martyrdom must run its
        course   10
Anyhow in a corner, some untidy spot
Where the dogs go on with their doggy life and the
        torturer's horse
Scratches its innocent behind on a tree.

In Brueghel's *Icarus*, for instance: how everything
        turns away
Quite leisurely from the disaster; the ploughman
        may
Have heard the splash, the forsaken cry,
But for him it was not an important failure; the sun
        shone
As it had to on the white legs disappearing into the
        green

Water; and the expensive delicate ship that must **have**
   seen
Something amazing, a boy falling out of the sky,   20
Had somewhere to get to and sailed calmly on.

The Novelist

Encased in talent like a uniform,
The rank of every poet is well known;
They can amaze us like a thunderstorm,
Or die so young, or live for years alone.

They can dash forward like hussars: but he
Must struggle out of his boyish gift and learn
How to be plain and awkward, how to be
One after whom none think it worth to turn.

For, to achieve his lightest wish, he must
Become the whole of boredom, subject to   10
Vulgar complaints like love, among the Just

Be just, among the Filthy filthy too,
And in his own weak person, if he can,
Must suffer dully all the wrongs of Man.

O Love, the interest itself in thoughtless Heaven

O Love, the interest itself in thoughtless Heaven,
Make simpler daily the beating of man's heart;
   within,

There in the ring where name and image meet,
Inspire them with such a longing as will make his
    thought
Alive like patterns a murmuration of starlings,
Rising in joy over wolds, unwittingly weave.

Here too on our little reef display your power,
This fortress perched on the edge of the Atlantic scarp,
The mole between all Europe and the exile-crowded
    sea;

And make us as Newton was who, in his garden
    watching   10
The apple falling towards England, became aware
Between himself and her of an eternal tie.

For now that dream which so long had contented our
    will,
I mean, of uniting the dead into a splendid empire,
Under whose fertilizing flood the Lancashire moss

Sprouted up chimneys, and Glamorgan hid a life
Grim as a tidal rock-pool's in its glove-shaped valleys,
Is already retreating into her maternal shadow;

Leaving the furnaces gasping in the impossible air,
That flotsam at which Dumbarton gapes and
    hungers;   20
While upon wind-loved Rowley no hammer shakes

The cluster of mounds like a midget golf-course,
    graves

Of some who created these intelligible dangerous
    marvels,
Affectionate people, but crude their sense of glory.

Far-sighted as falcons, they looked down another future;
For the seed in their loins were hostile though afraid
    of their pride,
And, tall with a shadow now, inertly wait.

In bar, in netted chicken-farm, in lighthouse,
Standing on these impoverished constricted acres,
The ladies and gentlemen apart, too much alone,   30

Consider the years of the measured world begun,
The barren virtuous marriage of stone and water.
Yet O, at this very moment of a hopeless sigh,

When, inland, they are thinking their thoughts but
    watching these islands
As children in Chester look to Moel Fammau to decide
On picnics by the clearness or withdrawal of her
    treeless crown.

Some possible dream, long coiled in the ammonite's
    slumber
Is uncurling, prepared to lay on our talk and reflection
Its military silence, its surgeon's idea of pain;

And out of the future into actual history,   40
As when Merlin, tamer of horses, and his lords to
    whom
Stonehenge was still a thought, the Pillars passed

And into the undared ocean swung north their prow
Drives through the night and star-concealing dawn
For the virgin roadsteads of our hearts an unwavering
    keel.

Lay your sleeping head, my love

Lay your sleeping head, my love,
Human on my faithless arm;
Time and fevers burn away
Individual beauty from
Thoughtful children, and the grave
Proves the child ephemeral:
But in my arms till break of day
Let the living creature lie,
Mortal, guilty, but to me
The entirely beautiful.   10

Soul and body have no bounds:
To lovers as they lie upon
Her tolerant enchanted slope
In their ordinary swoon,
Grave the vision Venus sends
Of supernatural sympathy,
Universal love and hope;
While an abstract insight wakes
Among the glaciers and the rocks
The hermit's sensual ecstasy.   20

Certainty, fidelity
On the stroke of midnight pass

Like vibrations of a bell
And fashionable madmen raise
Their pedantic boring cry:
Every farthing of the cost,
All the dreaded cards foretell,
Shall be paid, but from this night
Not a whisper, not a thought,
Not a kiss nor look be lost.   30

Beauty, midnight, vision dies:
Let the winds of dawn that blow
Softly round your dreaming head
Such a day of sweetness show
Eye and knocking heart may bless,
Find the mortal world enough;
Noons of dryness see you fed
By the involuntary powers,
Nights of insult let you pass
Watched by every human love.   40

Look, stranger, on this island now

Look, stranger, on this island now
The leaping light for your delight
    discovers,
Stand stable here
And silent be,
That through the channels of the ear
May wander like a river
The swaying sound of the sea.

Here at the small field's ending pause
When the chalk wall falls to the foam and its tall
    ledges
Oppose the pluck   10
And knock of the tide,
And the shingle scrambles after the suck-
    ing surf,
And the gull lodges
A moment on its sheer side.

Far off like floating seeds the ships
Diverge on urgent voluntary errands,
And the full view
Indeed may enter
And move in memory as now these clouds do,
That pass the harbour mirror   20
And all the summer through the water saunter.

1st September 1939

I sit in one of the dives
On Fifty-second Street
Uncertain and afraid
As the clever hopes expire
Of a low dishonest decade:
Waves of anger and fear
Circulate over the bright
And darkened lands of the earth,
Obsessing our private lives;
The unmentionable odour of death   10
Offends the September night.

Accurate scholarship can
Unearth the whole offence
From Luther until now
That has driven a culture mad,
Find what occurred at Linz,
What huge imago made
A psychopathic god:
I and the public know
What all schoolchildren learn,   20
Those to whom evil is done
Do evil in return.

Exiled Thucydides knew
All that a speech can say
About Democracy,
And what dictators do,
The elderly rubbish they talk
To an apathetic grave;
Analysed all in his book,
The enlightenment driven away,   30
The habit-forming pain,
Mismanagement and grief:
We must suffer them all again.

Into this neutral air
Where blind skyscrapers use
Their full height to proclaim
The strength of Collective Man,
Each language pours its vain
Competitive excuse:
But who can live for long   40
In an euphoric dream;

Out of the mirror they stare,
Imperialism's face
And the international wrong.

Faces along the bar
Cling to their average day:
The lights must never go out,
The music must always play,
All the conventions conspire
To make this fort assume   50
The furniture of home;
Lest we should see where we are,
Lost in a haunted wood,
Children afraid of the night
Who have never been happy or good.

The windiest militant trash
Important Persons shout
Is not so crude as our wish:
What mad Nijinsky wrote
About Diaghilev   60
Is true of the normal heart;
For the error bred in the bone
Of each woman and each man
Craves what it cannot have,
Not universal love
But to be loved alone.

From the conservative dark
Into the ethical life
The dense commuters come,
Repeating their morning vow;   70

"I *will* be true to the wife,
I'll concentrate more on my work,"
And helpless governors wake
To resume their compulsory game:
Who can release them now,
Who can reach the deaf,
Who can speak for the dumb?

All I have is a voice
To undo the folded lie,
The romantic lie in the brain   80
Of the sensual man-in-the-street
And the lie of Authority
Whose buildings grope the sky:
There is no such thing as the
    State
And no one exists alone;
Hunger allows no choice
To the citizen or the police;
We must love one another or die.

Defenceless under the night
Our world in stupor lies;   90
Yet, dotted everywhere,
Ironic points of light
Flash out wherever the Just
Exchange their messages:
May I, composed like them
Of Eros and of dust,
Beleaguered by the same
Negation and despair,
Show an affirming flame.

Streams

Dear water, clear water, playful in all your streams,
As you dash or loiter through life who does not love
      To sit beside you, to hear you and see you,
        Pure being, perfect in music and movement?

Air is boastful at times, earth slovenly, fire rude,
But you in your bearing are always immaculate,
      The most well-spoken of all the older
        Servants in the household of Mrs Nature.

Nobody suspects you of mocking him, for you still
Use the same vocables you were using the day   10
      Before that unexpected row which
        Downed every hod on half-finished Babel,

And still talk to yourself: nowhere are you disliked;
Arching your torso, you dive from a basalt sill,
      Canter across white chalk, slog forward
        Through red marls, the aboriginal pilgrim,

At home in all sections, but for whom we should be
Idolaters of a single rock, kept apart
      By our landscapes, excluding as alien
        The tales and diets of all other strata.   20

How could we love the absent one if you did not keep
Coming from a distance, or quite directly assist,
      As when past Iseult's tower you floated
        The willow pash-notes of wanted Tristram?

And *Homo Ludens*, surely, is your child, who make
Fun of our feuds by opposing identical banks,
      Transferring the loam from Huppim
        To Muppim and back each time you crankle.

Growth cannot add to your song: as unchristened
    brooks
Already you whisper to ants what, as Brahma's son, 30
      Descending his titanic staircase
        Into Assam, to Himalayan bears you thunder.

And not even man can spoil you: his company
Coarsens roses and dogs but, should he herd you
    through a sluice
      To toil at a turbine, or keep you
        Leaping in gardens for his amusement,

Innocent still is your outcry, water, and there
Even, to his soiled heart raging at what it is,
      Tells of a sort of world, quite other,
        Altogether different from this one   40

With its envies and passports, a polis like that
To which, in the names of scholars everywhere,
      Gaston Paris pledged his allegiance
        As Bismarck's siege-guns came within earshot.

Lately, in that dale of all Yorkshire's the loveliest,
Where, off its fell-side helter-skelter, Kisdon Beck
      Jumps into Swale with a boyish shouting,
        Sprawled out on grass, I dozed for a second,

And found myself following a croquet tournament
In a calm enclosure, with thrushes popular: 50
      Of all the players in that cool valley
    The best with the mallet was my darling.

While, on the wolds that begirdled it, wild old men
Hunted with spades and hammers, monomaniac each,
      For a megalith or a fossil,
    And bird-watchers stalked the mossy beech-
    woods.

Suddenly, over the lawn we started to run
For, lo, through the trees in a cream and golden coach
      Drawn by two baby locomotives,
    The god of mortal doting approached us,   60

Flanked by his bodyguard, those hardy armigers in
    green
Who laugh at thunderstorms and weep at a blue sky:
      He thanked us for our cheers of homage,
    And promised X and Y a passion undying.

With a wave of his torch he commanded a dance;
So round in a ring we flew, my dear on my right,
      When I awoke. But fortunate seemed that
    Day because of my dream and enlightened,

And dearer, water, than ever your voice, as if
Glad—though goodness knows why—to run with the
    human race,   70
      Wishing, I thought, the least of men their
    Figures of splendour, their holy places.

JOHN BETJEMAN (1906–)

Educated Marlborough and Magdalen College, Oxford. U.K. Press attaché, Dublin, 1941–43; Admiralty, 1944. Knighted 1969. Poet Laureate 1972. Works include: *Continual Dew* (1937); *An Oxford University Chest* (1938)–prose; *Old Lights for New Chancels* (1940); *New Bats in Old Belfries* (1945); *Selected Poems* (1948); *First and Last Loves* (1952)–prose; *A Few Late Chrysanthemums* (1954); *Collected Poems* (1958).

In this age, when the iron claws of 'progress' are gradually destroying the beauties of the past in landscape and architecture, an occasional voice in the wilderness cries out against the devastation. Such a voice is that of John Betjeman, lover of the past in house and hall, church and chapel, college and railway-station. In the apparently unpoetical—the drab suburb and the drab life of the suburbanite—he finds poetry. He observes sharply, notes minutely, and depicts wittily and satirically the second-rate in architecture and living. The blend of ancient and modern, of town and suburb and country, in contemporary English landscape (especially the Home Counties) is the subject he depicts with imagination, feeling, and sensitivity. "I love suburbs and gas-lights and Gothic Revival churches and mineral railways, provincial towns and garden cities." His poems recall with nostalgia the simple pleasures of his childhood and the simple architectural beauties of suburbia, the countryside, and the seaside. Here he is often a serious landscape artist in verse, who seeks his landscape in Lincolnshire, Hampshire, Cornwall, and in other counties that combine seaside and countryside.

Although his poems appear simple, their simplicity is deceptive and hides extreme technical skill employed on the most elementary of metres. His choice of words is as deliberately prosaic and ordinary as his choice of 'unpoetic' subject, and yet, from this combination, something very close to poetry, if not actually poetry, miraculously emerges.

Upper Lambourne

Up the ash-tree climbs the ivy,
    Up the ivy climbs the sun,
With a twenty-thousand pattering
    Has a valley breeze begun,
Feathery ash, neglected elder,
    Shift the shade and make it run—

Shift the shade toward the nettles,
    And the nettles set it free
To streak the stained Cararra headstone
    Where, in nineteen-twenty-three,   10
He who trained a hundred winners
    Paid the Final Entrance Fee.

Leathery limbs of Upper Lambourne,
    Leathery skin from sun and wind,
Leathery breeches, spreading stables,
    Shining saddles left behind—
To the down the string of horses
    Moving out of sight and mind.

Feathery ash in leathery Lambourne
    Waves above the sarsen stone,   20
And Edwardian plantations
    So coniferously moan
As to make the swelling downland,
    Far-surrounding, seem their own.

Greenaway

I know so well this turfy mile,
    These clumps of sea-pink withered brown,
The breezy cliff, the awkward stile,
    The sandy path that takes me down

To crackling layers of broken slate
    Where black and flat sea-woodlice crawl
And isolated rock pools wait
    Wash from the highest tides of all.

I know the roughly blasted track
    That skirts a small and smelly bay   10
And over squelching bladderwrack
    Leads to the beach at Greenaway.

Down on the shingle safe at last
    I hear the slowly dragging roar
As mighty rollers mount to cast
    Small coal and seaweed on the shore,

And spurting far as it can reach
    The shooting surf comes hissing round
To leave a line along the beach
    Of cowries waiting to be found.   20

Tide after tide by night and day
    The breakers battle with the land
And rounded smooth along the bay
    The faithful rocks protecting stand.

But in a dream the other night
    I saw this coastline from the sea
And felt the breakers plunging white
    Their weight of waters over me.

There were the stile, the turf, the shore,
    The safety line of shingle beach;   30
With every stroke I struck the more
    The backwash sucked me out of reach.

Back into what a water-world
    Of waving weed and waiting claws?
Of writhing tentacles uncurled
    To drag me to what dreadful jaws?

East Anglian Bathe

Oh when the early morning at the seaside
    Took us with hurrying steps from Horsey Mere
To see the whistling bent-grass on the leeside
    And then the tumbled breaker-line appear,
On high, the clouds with mighty adumbration
    Sailed over us to seaward fast and clear
And jellyfish in quivering isolation
    Lay silted in the dry sand of the breeze
And we, along the table-land of beach blown
    Went gooseflesh from our shoulders to our
        knees   10
And ran to catch the football, each to each thrown,
    In the soft and swirling music of the seas.

There splashed about our ankles as we waded
  Those intersecting wavelets morning-cold,
And sudden dark a patch of sea was shaded,
  And sudden light, another patch would hold
The warmth of whirling atoms in a sun-shot
  And underwater sandstorms green and gold.
So in we dived and louder than a gunshot
  Sea-water broke in fountains down the ear.   20
How cold the swim, how chattering cold the drying,
  How welcoming the inland reeds appear,
The wood-smoke and the breakfast and the frying,
  And your warm freshwater ripples, Horsey Mere.

Norfolk

How did the Devil come? When first attack?
  These Norfolk lanes recall lost innocence,
The years fall off and find me walking back
  Dragging a stick along the wooden fence
Down this same path, where, forty years ago,
My father strolled behind me, calm and slow.

I used to fill my hand with sorrel seeds
  And shower him with them from the tops of
   stiles,
I used to butt my head into his tweeds
  To make him hurry down those languorous
   miles   10
Of ash and alder-shaded lanes, till here
Our moorings and the masthead would appear.

There after supper lit by lantern light
    Warm in the cabin I could lie secure
And hear against the polished sides at night
    The lap lap lapping of the weedy Bure,
A whispering and watery Norfolk sound
Telling of all the moonlit reeds around,

How did the Devil come? When first attack?
    The church is just the same, though now I
        know   20
Fowler of Louth restored it. Time, bring back
    The rapturous ignorance of long ago,
The peace, before the dreadful daylight starts
Of unkept promises and broken hearts.

Essex

"The vagrant visitor erstwhile,"
    My colour-plate book says to me,
"Could wend by hedgerow-side and stile,
    From Benfleet down to Leigh-on-Sea."

And as I turn the colour-plates
    Edwardian Essex opens wide,
Mirrored in ponds and seen through gates,
    Sweet uneventful countryside.

Like streams the little by-roads run
    Through oats and barley round a hill   10
To where blue willows catch the sun
    By some white weather-boarded mill.

"A Summer Idyll Matching Tye"
    "At Havering-atte-Bower the Stocks"
And cobbled pathways lead the eye
    To cottage doors and hollyhocks.

Far Essex,—fifty miles away
    The level wastes of sucking mud
Where distant barges high with hay
    Come sailing in upon the flood.   20

Near Essex of the River Lea
    And anglers out with hook and worm
And Epping Forest glades where we
    Had beanfeasts with my father's firm.

At huge and convoluted pubs
    They used to set us down from brakes
In that half-land of football clubs
    Which London near the Forest makes.

Then deepest Essex few explore
    Where steepest thatch is sunk in flowers   30
And out of elm and sycamore
    Rise flinty fifteenth-century towers.

I see the little branch line go
    By white farms roofed in red and brown,
The old Great Eastern winding slow
    To some forgotten country town.

Now yarrow chokes the railway track,
  Brambles obliterate the stile,
No motor coach can take me back
  To that Edwardian 'erstwhile.'   40

A Child Ill

Oh, little body, do not die.
  The soul looks out through wide blue eyes
So questioningly into mine,
  That my tormented soul replies:
"Oh, little body, do not die.
  You hold the soul that talks to me
Although our conversation be
  As wordless as the windy sky."

So looked my father at the last
  Right in my soul, before he died,   10
Though words we spoke went heedless past
  As London traffic-roar outside.
And now the same blue eyes I see
  Look through me from a little son,
So questioning, so searchingly
  That youthfulness and age are one.

My father looked at me and died
  Before my soul made full reply.
Lord, leave this other Light alight—
  Oh, little body, do not die.   20

Before the Anæsthetic
or
A Real Fright

Intolerably sad, profound
St Giles's bells are ringing round,
They bring the slanting summer rain
To tap the chestnut boughs again
Whose shadowy cave of rainy leaves
The gusty belfry-song receives.
Intolerably sad and true,
Victorian red and jewel blue,
The mellow bells are ringing round
And charge the evening light with sound,   10
And I look motionless from bed
On heavy trees and purple red
And hear the midland bricks and tiles
Throw back the bells of stone St Giles,
Bells, ancient now as castle walls,
Now hard and new as pitchpine stalls,
Now full with help from ages past,
Now dull with death and hell at last.
Swing up! and give me hope of life,
Swing down! and plunge the surgeon's knife.   20
I, breathing for a moment, see
Death wing himself away from me
And think, as on this bed I lie,
Is it extinction when I die?
I move my limbs and use my sight;
Not yet, thank God, not yet the Night.

Oh better far those echoing hells
Half-threaten'd in the pealing bells
Than that this "I" should cease to be—
Come quickly, Lord, come quick to me.   30
St Giles's bells are asking now
"And hast thou known the Lord, hast thou?"
St Giles's bells, they richly ring
"And was that Lord our Christ the King?"
St Giles's bells they hear me call
I never knew the Lord at all.
Oh not in me your Saviour dwells
You ancient, rich St Giles's bells.
Illuminated missals—spires—
Wide screens and decorated quires—   40
All these I loved, and on my knees
I thanked myself for knowing these
And watched the morning sunlight pass
Through richly stained Victorian glass
And in the colour-shafted air
I, kneeling, thought the Lord was there.
Now, lying in the gathering mist
I know that Lord did not exist;
Now, lest this "I" should cease to be,
Come, real Lord, come quick to me.   50
With every gust the chestnut sighs,
With every breath a mortal dies;
The man who smiled alone, alone,
And went his journey on his own
With "Will you give my wife this letter,
In case, of course, I don't get better?"
Waits for his coffin lid to close
On waxen head and yellow toes.

Almighty Saviour, had I Faith
There'd be no fight with kindly Death.   60
Intolerably long and deep
St Giles's bells swing on in sleep:
"But still you go from here alone"
Say all the bells about the Throne.

WALTER DE LA MARE (1873–1956)
C.H., 1948; O.M., 1953.

Born in Charlton, Kent. Educated St Paul's Cathedral
Choir School, London. Spent eighteen years in commercial life before, in 1908, devoting his time to
literature. His first book (*Songs of Childhood*, 1902) was
published under the name of Walter Ramal, but his
second (*Henry Brocken*, 1904—a prose romance)
appeared under his own name. Awarded a Civil List
pension for the distinction of his literary work. Works
include: *Poems* (1906); *The Return* (1910)—awarded
the Polignac Prize (1911); *The Listeners* (1912);
Collected Poems (1920); *Memoirs of a Midget* (1921)—
fiction—awarded the James Tait Black Prize; *Come
Hither* (1923)—an anthology; *The Fleeting and other
Poems* (1933); *Memory and other Poems* (1938); *Behold,
This Dreamer* (1939)—an anthology; *The Burning Glass*
(1945); *The Traveller* (1946); *Inward Companion* (1950);
Winged Chariot (1951); *O Lovely England* (1953); *Private
View* (1953)—criticism; *A Beginning* (1956)—fiction.

"Between children's dreams and their reality looms
no impassable abyss," writes Walter de la Mare; his
poetry crosses this abyss and brings to our eyes and
ears another world—a world beyond Time, a world
lying just beyond this one, and seen in moments of
vision, more especially by children and poets. To enter
this kingdom one must "become as a child," as Blake
did when he wrote his *Songs of Innocence*. One must be
simple and humble, faithful and loving, filled with
wonder and awe, and ready to accept the miracle. As
much at home in this shadowy beyond-world as in the

ordinary world, de la Mare is ever conscious of its
presence and ever ready to slip over its boundary. As
he says, "One may voyage far and perhaps in another
Real." It is a world more real than this and eternal;
children inhabit it with ease, naturalness, and un-
consciousness, and poets and visionaries, like Blake
and Traherne, catch glimpses of its wonder and delight. But this world is not all beauty: there is fear in it,
and terror, and helplessness, and evil, and, above all,
mystery. Dream is one way of entry into this world;
death is another. Death is not nothingness; it may be a
state in which we know other things—and perhaps
lovelier things. Knowing this other world to be so near
makes every moment of living exciting, lest every
moment should be the last:

> Look thy last on all things lovely,
> Every hour.

In the quietest and gentlest of rhythms, never
obtrusive but always in harmony, with the simplest
and subtlest of metres, de la Mare takes us by the hand
into this elusive land where a footfall is a whisper and
a whisper is a revelation. We overhear snatches of
conversation whose undertones we do not understand
with our intellect but with our senses. The poet dwells
there; we are visitors, intruders, only the child in us
giving us the right of entry into this world of new
facts and reality, where are intensified the everyday
emotions of joy and sorrow, hope and fear.

The other unfailing subject of de la Mare's poetry is
England and its traditions. The ordinary phenomena
of life here—the seasons, flowers, birds, trees, animals,
the cycle of life and death—find new interpretations in
his poetry, which makes the familiar new and more
beautiful, and at the same time sees the divinity behind

it. For everything is seen with the eye of love and keen observation, except the modern world of science, which is uncongenial to him. One of his last poems foresees the clever analysts of to-day destroying the world in their endeavour to see how it is made:

> Not to find joy in what it is *for*,
>   But merely what made *of*.

But, although he finds this modern world alien to his spirit, as a poet he is drawn to contemplate and sympathize with the plight of those entangled in it.

In *A Tribute to Walter de la Mare on his 75th Birthday*, various contributors discussed the poet and his work. The following lines are part of T. S. Eliot's tribute:

> By whom, and by what means, was this designed?
> The whispered incantation which allows
> Free passage to the phantoms of the mind.
>
> By you; by those deceptive cadences
> Wherewith the common measure is refined;
> By conscious art practised with natural ease. . . .
>
>   Or when the lawn
> Is pressed by unseen feet, and ghosts return
> Gently at twilight, gently at dawn,
>
> The sad intangible who grieve and yearn;
> When the familiar scene is suddenly strange
> Or the well known is what we have to learn,
> And two worlds meet, and intersect, and change.

The Listeners

"Is there anybody there?" said the Traveller,
    Knocking on the moonlit door;
And his horse in the silence champed the grasses
    Of the forest's ferny floor:
And a bird flew up out of the turret,
    Above the Traveller's head:
And he smote upon the door again a second
        time;
    "Is there anybody there?" he said.
But no one descended to the Traveller;
    No head from the leaf-fringed sill   10
Leaned over and looked into his grey eyes,
    Where he stood perplexed and still.
But only a host of phantom listeners
    That dwelt in the lone house then
Stood listening in the quiet of the moonlight
    To that voice from the world of men:
Stood thronging the faint moonbeams on the dark
        stair,
    That goes down to the empty hall,
Hearkening in an air stirred and shaken
    By the lonely Traveller's call.   20
And he felt in his heart their strangeness,
    Their stillness answering his cry,
While his horse moved, cropping the dark turf,
    'Neath the starred and leafy sky;
For he suddenly smote on the door, even
    Louder, and lifted his head:—

"Tell them I came, and no one answered,
    That I kept my word," he said.
Never the least stir made the listeners,
    Though every word he spake   30
Fell echoing through the shadowiness of the still
        house
    From the one man left awake:
Ay, they heard his foot upon the stirrup,
    And the sound of iron on stone,
And how the silence surged softly backward,
    When the plunging hoofs were gone.

The Ghost

"Who knocks?" "I, who was beautiful,
    Beyond all dreams to restore,
I, from the roots of the dark thorn am hither,
    And knock on the door."

"Who speaks?" "I—once was my speech
    Sweet as the bird's on the air,
When echo lurks by the waters to heed;
    'Tis I speak thee fair."

"Dark is the hour!" "Ay, and cold."
    "Lone is my house." "Ah, but mine?"   10
"Sight, touch, lips, eyes yearned in vain."
    "Long dead these to thine . . . ."

Silence. Still faint on the porch
    Brake the flames of the stars.

In gloom groped a hope-wearied hand
  Over keys, bolts, and bars.

A face peered. All the grey night
  In chaos of vacancy shone;
Nought but vast sorrow was there—
  The sweet cheat gone.   20

Haunted

The rabbit in his burrow keeps
No guarded watch, in peace he sleeps;
The wolf that howls in challenging night
Cowers to her lair at morning light;
The simplest bird entwines a nest
Where she may lean her lovely breast,
Couched in the silence of the bough:—
But thou, O man, what rest hast thou?

Thy emptiest solitude can bring
Only a subtler questioning   10
In thy divided heart. Thy bed
Recalls at dawn what midnight said.
Seek how thou wilt to feign content,
Thy flaming ardour's quickly spent;
Soon thy last company is gone,
And leaves thee—with thyself—alone.

Pomp and great friends may hem thee round,
A thousand busy tasks be found;

Earth's thronging beauties may beguile
Thy longing lovesick heart awhile;   20
And pride, like clouds of sunset, spread
A changing glory round thy head;
But fade will all; and thou must come,
Hating thy journey, homeless, home.

Rave how thou wilt; unmoved, remote,
That inward presence slumbers not,
Frets out each secret from thy breast,
Gives thee no rally, pause, nor rest,
Scans close thy very thoughts, lest they
Should sap his patient power away;   30
Answers thy wrath with peace, thy cry
With tenderest taciturnity.

Go far; come near

Go far; come near;
You still must be
The centre of your own small mystery.
Range body and soul—
Gone on to further goal,
Still shall you find
At end, nought else but *thee*.
Oh, in what straitened bounds
Of thought and aim—
And even sights and sounds—   10
Your earthly lot is doomed to stay!

And yet, your smallest whim
By secret grace
To look the simplest flower in the face
Gives an inevitable reflection back,
Not of your own self only,
But of one
Who, having achieved its miracle,
Rests there, and is not gone;
Who still o'er your own darker deeps holds sway   20
Into whatever shallows you may stray.

Whatever quicksands loom before you yet,—
Indifference, the endeavour to forget,
Whatever truce for which your soul may yearn,
Gives you but smaller room
In which to turn,
Until you reach the haven
Of the tomb.

"The haven?" Count the chances. . . . Is that so?
You are your Universe. Could death's quick dart   30
Be aimed at aught less mortal than the heart?
Could body's end,
Whereto it soon shall go,
Be end of all you mean, and are, my friend?

Ah, when clocks stop, and no-more-time begins,
May he who gave the flower
Its matchless hour,
And you the power
To win the love that only loving wins,
Have mercy on your miseries and your sins.   40

Fare Well

When I lie where shades of darkness
Shall no more assail mine eyes,
Nor the rain make lamentation
    When the wind sighs;
How will fare the world whose wonder
Was the very proof of me?
Memory fades, must the remembered
    Perishing be?

Oh, when this my dust surrenders
Hand, foot, lip, to dust again,   10
May these loved and loving faces
    Please other men!
May the rusting harvest hedgerow
Still the Traveller's Joy entwine,
And as happy children gather
    Posies once mine.

Look thy last on all things lovely,
Every hour. Let no night
Seal thy sense in deathly slumber
    Till to delight   20
Thou have paid thy utmost blessing;
Since that all things thou wouldst praise
Beauty took from those who loved them
    In other days.

All That's Past

Very old are the woods;
　　And the buds that break
Out of the brier's boughs,
　　When March winds wake,
So old with their beauty are—
　　Oh, no man knows
Through what wild centuries
　　Roves back the rose.

Very old are the brooks;
　　And the rills that rise   10
Where snow sleeps cold beneath
　　The azure skies
Sing such a history
　　Of come and gone,
Their every drop is as wise
　　As Solomon.

Very old are we men;
　　Our dreams are tales
Told in dim Eden
　　By Eve's nightingales;   20
We wake and whisper awhile,
　　But, the day gone by,
Silence and sleep like fields
　　Of amaranth lie.

Absence

"What, autumn, friend! And she not yet back?
The year is old, past her equinox;
Now, with their winds, come the tardier nights,
The laggarding mornings!"—Memory mocks.

"So the harvest moon may rise in vain
On one whom of old it could tranquillise
Merely by lighting his heavens. Alas,
How coldly then it will meet his eyes!

"Once-dear September: its sheaves and dew,
Seeding grasses . . . evening peace!　　10
Strange, is it not, that things like these
May shed so ironic a tenderness?

"Absence will meet you everywhere—
Mute lips, dark eyes, and phantom brow.
I warned you not to invite in ghosts;
No power have I to evict them now.

"Yet the wildest longings, they say, burn down;
Wasted, as a candle its wax; are passed. . . ."
Thus Memory taunts me, wishing me well!—
With, "There's one Goodbye *must* be the last."　　20

The Spark

Calm was the evening, as if asleep,
But sickled on high with brooding storm,
Couched in invisible space. And, lo!
I saw in utter silence sweep
Out of that darkening starless vault
A gliding spark, as blanched as snow,
That burned into dust, and vanished in
A hay-cropped meadow, brightly green.

A meteor from the cold of space,
Lost in Earth's wilderness of air?—   10
Presage of lightnings soon to shine
In splendour on this lonely place?—
I cannot tell; but only how fair
It glowed within the crystalline
Pure heavens, and of its strangeness lit
My mind to joy at sight of it.

Yet what is common as lovely may be:
The petalled daisy, a honey bell,
A pebble, a branch of moss, a gem
Of dew, or fallen rain—if we   20
A moment in their beauty dwell;
Entranced, alone, see only them.
How blind to wait, till, merely unique,
Some omen thus the all bespeak!

The Snowdrop

Now—now, as low I stooped, thought I,
I will see what this snowdrop *is*;
So shall I put much argument by,
    And solve a lifetime's mysteries.

A northern wind had frozen the grass;
Its blades were hoar with crystal rime,
Aglint like light-dissecting glass
    At beam of morning-prime.

From hidden bulb the flower reared up
Its angled, slender, cold, dark stem,   10
Whence dangled an inverted cup
    For tri-leaved diadem.

Beneath these ice-pure sepals lay
A triplet of green-pencilled snow,
Which in the chill-aired gloom of day
    Stirred softly to and fro.

Mind fixed, but else made vacant, I,
Lost to my body, called my soul
To don that frail solemnity,
    Its inmost self my goal.   20

And though in vain—no mortal mind
Across that threshold yet hath fared!—
In this collusion I divined
    Some consciousness we shared.

Strange roads—while suns, a myriad, set—
Had led us through infinity;
And where they crossed, there then had met
Not two of us, but three.

Polonius

There haunts in Time's bare house an active ghost,
Enamoured of his name, Polonius.
He moves small fingers much, and all his speech
Is like a sampler of precisest words,
Set in the pattern of a simpleton.
His mirth floats eerily down chill corridors;
His sigh—it is a sound that loves a keyhole;
His tenderness a faint court-tarnished thing;
His wisdom prates as from a wicker cage;
His very belly is a pompous nought;   10
His eye a page that hath forgot his errand.
Yet in his bran—his spiritual bran—
Lies hid a child's demure, small, silver whistle
Which, to his horror, God blows, unawares,
And sets men staring. It is sad to think,
Might he but don indeed thin flesh and blood,
And pace important to Law's inmost room,
He would see, much marvelling, one immensely wise,
Named Bacon, who, at sound of his youth's step,
Would turn and call him Cousin—for the likeness. 20

A Portrait

Old: yet unchanged;—still pottering in his thoughts;
Still eagerly enslaved by books and print;
Less plagued, perhaps, by rigid musts and oughts,
But no less frantic in vain argument;

Still happy as a child, with its small toys,
Over his inkpot and his bits and pieces,—
Life's arduous, fragile and ingenuous joys,
Whose charm failed never—nay, it even increases!

Ev'n happier in watch of bird or flower,
Rainbow in heaven, or bud on thorny spray,   10
A star-strewn nightfall, and that heart-break hour
Of sleep-drowsed senses between dawn and day;

Loving the light—laved eyes in those wild hues!—
And dryad twilight, and the thronging dark;
A Crusoe ravished by mere solitude—
And silence—edged with music's faintest *Hark*!

And any chance-seen face whose loveliness
Hovers, a mystery, between dream and real;
Things usual yet miraculous that bless
And overwell a heart that still can feel;   20

Haunted by questions no man answered yet;
Pining to leap from A clean on to Z;
Absorbed by problems which the wise forget;
Avid for fantasy—yet how staid a head!

Senses at daggers with his intellect;
Quick, stupid; vain, retiring; ardent, cold;
Faithful and fickle; rash and circumspect;
And never yet at rest in any fold;

Punctual at meals; a spendthrift, close as Scot;
Rebellious, tractable, childish—long gone grey!   30
Impatient, volatile, tongue wearying not—
Loose, too: which, yet, thank heaven, was taught to
    pray;

"Childish" indeed!—a waif on shingle shelf
Fronting the rippled sands, the sun, the sea;
And nought but his marooned precarious self
For questing consciousness and will-to-be;

A feeble venturer—in a world so wide!
So rich in action, daring, cunning, strife!
You'd think, poor soul, he had taken Sloth for
    bride,—
Unless the imagined is the breath of life;   40

Unless to speculate bring virgin gold,
And *Let's-pretend* can range the seven seas,
And dreams are not mere tales by idiot told,
And tongueless truth may hide in fantasies;

Unless the alone may their own company find,
And churchyards harbour phantoms 'mid their bones,
And even a daisy may suffice a mind
Whose bindweed can redeem a heap of stones;

Too frail a basket for so many eggs—
Loose-woven: Gosling? cygnet? Laugh or weep? 50
Or is the cup at richest in its dregs?
The actual realest on the verge of sleep?

One yet how often the prey of doubt and fear,
Of bleak despondence, stark anxiety;
Ardent for what is neither now nor here,
An Orpheus fainting for Eurydice;

Not yet inert, but with a tortured breast
At hint of that bleak gulf—his last farewell;
Pining for peace, assurance, pause and rest,
Yet slave to what he loves past words to tell; 60

A foolish, fond old man, his bed-time nigh,
Who still at western windows stays to win
A transient respite from the latening sky,
And scarce can bear it when the Sun goes in.

T. S. ELIOT (1888–1965)
O.M., 1948.

Born at St Louis, Missouri, of an old New England family. Educated Harvard University, the Sorbonne, and Merton College, Oxford. In 1914 he settled in London, which became his home for life—he was naturalized in 1927. For a time he was Assistant Editor of *The Egoist*, and helped to found *The Criterion*, which he edited. Charles Eliot Norton Professor of Poetry, Harvard University, 1932–33. Awarded Nobel Prize for Literature, 1948. Director of the publishers Faber and Faber, Ltd. Works include: *Prufrock and Other Observations* (1917); *Poems* (1919); *The Sacred Wood* (1920)—criticism; *The Waste Land* (1922); *Poems* (1925); *Ash Wednesday* (1930); *The Rock* (1934)—a pageant-play; *Murder in the Cathedral* (1935)—a play; *Collected Poems* (1936); *Essays Ancient and Modern* (1936); *The Family Reunion* (1939)—a verse-play; *Four Quartets* (1944); *The Cocktail Party* (1950)—a verse-play; *The Confidential Clerk* (1954)—a play; *On Poetry and Poets* (1957)—essays; *The Elder Statesman* (1958)—a play; *Collected Poems, 1909–1962*, (1963).

The publication of *The Waste Land* in 1922 was an event in English poetry as epoch-making as the publication of *Lyrical Ballads* in 1798. Both books rejected the out-worn conventions in poetry of the past century, and both used ordinary speech to convey the poet's feelings. Apparently turning its back on all that is traditional in English poetry, *The Waste Land* yet carries out Eliot's conception of poetry as "a living whole of all the poetry that has ever been written," and of a mature poet as "one who in his poetry retwines as

many straying strands of tradition as possible." Eliot
has deliberately made the poetry of the past part of his
own poetry. Using fragments of the great poetry of the
past to contrast the spacious days of old with the
degradation, decadence, sterility, and lack of a sense of
direction of his own days, Eliot has succeeded in
expressing with finality the sense of futility, cynical
bitterness, and disillusionment experienced in the years
after the First World War, though he himself has dis-
claimed this intention and said that others have found
in the poem only their own "illusion of disillusionment"; he himself has found in this "heap of broken
images" a possibility of hope.

Eliot justifies his allusive, oblique style of that
period, and later, in his essay on *The Metaphysical Poets*:

> The poets of our time must be different. Our civiliza-
> tion is very complex and varied, and this variety and
> complexity, operating on our refined sensations, must
> give rise to varied and complex results. The poet has
> to become always more *compressed*, more allusive, more
> indirect, even doing violence to language in order to
> express himself.

Through his various plays from *Murder in the Cathedral*
to *The Confidential Clerk*, Eliot has tended in his poetry,
as in his life, to accept the authority of tradition and of
religion as the only means to save us from the chaos
that has gradually overwhelmed man since the end of
the nineteenth century through his materialism and his
lack of spiritual standards. His conversion to Anglo-
Catholicism is one of the aspects of his pursuit of
religious experience and certitude. His criticism of
contemporary life ("I have measured out my life with
coffee spoons") with its rejection of the spiritual is
part of his religious conviction that the spiritual truth
is the highest truth. It is finally in *Four Quartets* (the

first of them, *Burnt Norton*, was published as far back as 1935) that Eliot sets down his inmost convictions about life and death, time and eternity, faith and reason.

Eliot's debt to earlier writers does not end with the quotations from them incorporated in his own verse. Two writers among many may be mentioned. Frequent mention of Dante in both his poetry and his critical writings suggests his admiration of him; with both writers diction is precise and visual images clear, style is simple and the use of words economical. With the English metaphysical poets, and especially Donne, he shares a feeling of the disintegration and collapse of our civilization, and both he and Donne are searching for a certitude not to be found in the science of their own day. Both have the courage to face reality in its most horrible and degrading aspects as well as in the beautiful, and both diagnose and analyse and express with irony their reactions to the new thought and the new knowledge. No aspect of life is too sordid or too commonplace to be described in their poetry. To Donne, especially, he owes much in the use of technical devices—the colloquial, familiar tone, the conversational and yet startling vocabulary, the rapid association of ideas, the wit of 'conceits'—the unexpected contrasts that give the sensation of life as it is lived.

That at which I have long aimed, in writing poetry; to write poetry which should be essentially poetry, with nothing poetic about it, poetry standing naked in its bare bones, or poetry so transparent that we should not see the poetry, but that which we are meant to see through the poetry, poetry so transparent that in reading it we are intent on what the poem *points at*, and not on the poetry, this seems to me the thing to try for.

T. S. ELIOT

"A cold coming we had of it,
Just the worst time of the year
For a journey, and such a long journey:
The ways deep and the weather sharp,
The very dead of winter."
And the camels galled, sore-footed, refractory,
Lying down in the melting snow.
There were times we regretted
The summer palaces on slopes, the terraces,
And the silken girls bringing sherbet.   10
Then the camel men cursing and grumbling
And running away, and wanting their liquor and
    women,
And the night-fires going out, and the lack of
    shelters,
And the cities hostile and the towns unfriendly
And the villages dirty and charging high prices:
A hard time we had of it.
At the end we preferred to travel all night,
Sleeping in snatches,
With the voices singing in our ears, saying
That this was all folly.   20

Then at dawn we came down to a temperate valley,
Wet, below the snow line, smelling of vegetation;
With a running stream and a water-mill beating the
    darkness,
And three trees on the low sky,

And an old white horse galloped away in the
    meadow.
Then we came to a tavern with vine-leaves over the
    lintel,
Six hands at an open door dicing for pieces of
    silver,
And feet kicking the empty wine-skins.
But there was no information, and so we continued
And arrived at evening, not a moment too soon   30
Finding the place; it was (you may say) satisfactory.

All this was a long time ago, I remember,
And I would do it again, but set down
This set down
This: were we led all that way for
Birth or Death? There was a birth, certainly,
We had evidence and no doubt. I had seen birth
    and death,
But had thought they were different, this Birth was
Hard and bitter agony for us, like Death, our death.
We returned to our places, these Kingdoms,   40
But no longer at ease here, in the old dispensation,
With an alien people clutching their gods.
I should be glad of another death.

Animula

"Issues from the hand of God, the simple soul"
To a flat world of changing lights and noise,
To light, dark, dry or damp, chilly or warm;
Moving between the legs of tables and of chairs,

Rising or falling, grasping at kisses and toys,
Advancing boldly, sudden to take alarm,
Returning to the corner of arm and knee,
Eager to be reassured, taking pleasure
In the fragrant brilliance of the Christmas tree,
Pleasure in the wind, the sunlight and the sea;   10
Studies the sunlit pattern on the floor
And running stags around a silver tray;
Confounds the actual and the fanciful,
Content with playing-cards and kings and queens,
What the fairies do and what the servants say.
The heavy burden of the growing soul
Perplexes and offends more, day by day;
Week by week, offendes and perplexes more
With the imperatives of "is and seems"
And may and may not, desire and control.   20
The pain of living and the drug of dreams
Curl up the small soul in the window seat
Behind the *Encyclopædia Britannica*.
Issues from the hand of time the simple soul
Irresolute and selfish, misshapen, lame,
Unable to fare forward or retreat,
Fearing the warm reality, the offered good,
Denying the importunity of the blood,
Shadow of its own shadows, spectre in its own
    gloom,
Leaving disordered papers in a dusty room;   30
Living first in the silence after the viaticum.

Pray for Guitteriez, avid for speed and power,
For Boudin, blown to pieces,
For this one who made a great fortune,

And that one who went his own way.
Pray for Floret, by the boarhound slain between the
    yew trees,
Pray for us now and at the hour of our birth.

The Love Song of J. Alfred Prufrock

> *S'io credesse che mia risposta fosse*
> *A persona che mai tornasse al mondo,*
> *Questa fiamma staria senza piu scosse.*
> *Ma perciocche giammai di questo fondo*
> *Non torno vivo alcun, s'i'odo el vero,*
> *Senza tema d'infamia ti rispondo.*

Let us go then, you and I,
When the evening is spread out against the sky
Like a patient etherised upon a table;
Let us go, through certain half-deserted streets,
The muttering retreats
Of restless nights in one-night cheap hotels
And sawdust restaurants with oyster-shells:
Streets that follow like a tedious argument
Of insidious intent
To lead you to an overwhelming question. . . .   10
Oh, do not ask, "What is it?"
Let us go and make our visit.

In the room the women come and go
Talking of Michelangelo.

The yellow fog that rubs its back upon the window-
    panes,

The yellow smoke that rubs its muzzle on the window-
    panes
Licked its tongue into the corners of the evening,
Lingered upon the pools that stand in drains,
Let fall upon its back the soot that falls from
    chimneys,
Slipped by the terrace, made a sudden leap,   20
And seeing that it was a soft October night,
Curled once about the house, and fell asleep.

And indeed there will be time
For the yellow smoke that slides along the street
Rubbing its back upon the window-panes;
There will be time, there will be time
To prepare a face to meet the faces that you
    meet;
There will be time to murder and create,
And time for all the works and days of hands
That lift and drop a question on your plate;   30
Time for you and time for me,
And time yet for a hundred indecisions,
And for a hundred visions and revisions,
Before the taking of a toast and tea.

In the room the women come and go
Talking of Michelangelo.

And indeed there will be time
To wonder, "Do I dare?" and, "Do I dare?"
Time to turn back and descend the stair,
With a bald spot in the middle of my hair—   40
(They will say: "How his hair is growing thin!")

My morning coat, my collar mounting firmly to the
    chin,
My necktie rich and modest, but asserted by a simple
    pin—
(They will say: "But how his arms and legs are
    thin!")
Do I dare
Disturb the universe?
In a minute there is time
For decisions and revisions which a minute will
    reverse.

For I have known them all already, known them
    all—
Have known the evenings, mornings, afternoons,   50
I have measured out my life with coffee spoons;
I know the voices dying with a dying fall
Beneath the music from a farther room.
      So how should I presume?

And I have known the eyes already, known them
    all—
The eyes that fix you in a formulated phrase,
And when I am formulated, sprawling on a pin,
When I am pinned and wriggling on the wall,
Then how should I begin
To spit out all the butt-ends of my days and ways? 60
      And how should I presume?

And I have known the arms already, known them
    all—
Arms that are braceleted and white and bare

(But in the lamplight, downed with light brown
     hair!)
Is it perfume from a dress
That makes me so digress?
Arms that lie along a table, or wrap about a shawl.
     And should I then presume?
     And how should I begin?

       . . . . . .

Shall I say, I have gone at dusk through narrow
     streets   70
And watched the smoke that rises from the pipes
Of lonely men in shirt-sleeves, leaning out of
     windows? . . .

I should have been a pair of ragged claws
Scuttling across the floors of silent seas.

       . . . . . .

And the afternoon, the evening, sleeps so peacefully!
Smoothed by long fingers,
Asleep . . . tired . . . or it malingers,
Stretched on the floor, here beside you and me.
Should I, after tea and cakes and ices,
Have the strength to force the moment to its crisis? 80
But though I have wept and fasted, wept and prayed,
Though I have seen my head (grown slightly bald)
     brought in upon a platter,
I am no prophet—and here's no great matter;
I have seen the moment of my greatness flicker,
And I have seen the eternal Footman hold my coat,
     and snicker,
And in short, I was afraid.

And would it have been worth it, after all,
After the cups, the marmalade, the tea,
Among the porcelain, among some talk of you and
    me,
Would it have been worth while,   90
To have bitten off the matter with a smile,
To have squeezed the universe into a ball
To roll it toward some overwhelming question,
To say: "I am Lazarus, come from the dead,
Come back to tell you all, I shall tell you all"—
If one, settling a pillow by her head,
      Should say: "That is not what I meant at all:
      That is not it, at all."

And would it have been worth it, after all,
Would it have been worth while,   100
After the sunsets and the dooryards and the sprinkled
    streets,
After the novels, after the teacups, after the skirts
    that trail along the floor—
And this, and so much more?—
It is impossible to say just what I mean!
But as if a magic lantern threw the nerves in patterns
    on a screen:
Would it have been worth while
If one, settling a pillow or throwing off a shawl,
And, turning toward the window, should say:
      "That is not it at all,
      That is not what I meant, at all."   110

     •   •   •   •   •   •

No, I am not Prince Hamlet, nor was meant to be;
Am an attendant lord, one that will do
To swell a progress, start a scene or two,
Advise the prince; no doubt, an easy tool,
Deferential, glad to be of use,
Politic, cautious, and meticulous;
Full of high sentence, but a bit obtuse;
At times, indeed, almost ridiculous—
Almost, at times, the Fool.

I grow old. . . . I grow old. . . .   120
I shall wear the bottoms of my trousers rolled.

Shall I part my hair behind? Do I dare to eat a peach?
I shall wear white flannel trousers, and walk upon
      the beach.
I have heard the mermaids singing, each to each.

I do not think that they will sing to me.

I have seen them riding seaward on the waves
Combing the white hair of the waves blown back
When the wind blows the water white and black.

We have lingered in the chambers of the sea
By sea-girls wreathed with seaweed red and brown 130
Till human voices wake us, and we drown.

ROBERT FROST (1874–1963)

American poet. Born in San Francisco. Educated Dartmouth and Harvard University. He moved at an early age to New England. From 1911 to 1915 he lived in England, where his first book was published. Returning to the United States he devoted himself to poetry and teaching. Awarded the Pulitzer Prize for Poetry 1924, 1931, 1937, 1943. Works include: *A Boy's Will* (1913); *North of Boston* (1914); *Mountain Interval* (1916); *New Hampshire* (1923); *West-running Brook* (1928); *Collected Poems* (1930 and 1933); *A Further Range* (1936); *A Witness Tree* (1942); *Steeple Bush* (1947); *Selected Poems* (1955).

"A poem begins in delight and ends in wisdom." When Frost wrote this he was thinking of his own poems and describing them exactly as they are. From 1911 to 1915 he was a friend and neighbour in Gloucestershire of Wilfrid Gibson, Lascelles Abercrombie, and John Drinkwater.

> Robert Frost kept on and on and on,
> In his slow New England fashion, for our delight,
> Holding us with shrewd turns and racy quips,
> And the rare twinkle of his grave blue eyes. . . .
>   Frost's rich and ripe philosophy,
> That had the body and tang of good draught-cider,
> And poured as clear a stream.
>
>   WILFRID GIBSON, *The Golden Room*

It was at this time that Frost made Edward Thomas turn to poetry and become a poet by suggesting that "he was writing as good poetry as anybody alive, but in prose form where it did not declare itself, and gain him recognition. I referred him to paragraphs in his book, *The Pursuit of Spring*, and told him to write it in verse in exactly the same cadence. That is all there was to it. His poetry declared itself in verse form." (Robert Frost, in a letter.) In 1915 Frost returned to America and settled in where he had previously farmed—New Hampshire, which he has lovingly depicted in his poems with the simplicity, fidelity, and insight of a Wordsworth and with the humour that Wordsworth lacked.

Frost is essentially a traditionalist and a regional poet. In the simplest of language, with the cadences and vocabulary of ordinary speech, with a disarming simplicity and ease and spontaneity (which are the result of much study and experiment—"a careful casualness"), Frost can turn out a phrase that remains in the mind with the racy tang and inevitability of a proverb.

> Good fences make good neighbours.

> Home is the place, where, when you have to go there, They have to take you in.

> We love the things we love for what they are.

> Most of the change we think we see in life Is due to truths being in and out of favour.

The whole landscape of New Hampshire and Vermont, its activities, its animals, domestic and wild, its birds, its insects, are open to his observant eye as he strolls leisurely—apple-picking, mowing, mending walls, ploughing, whetting a scythe, wild grapes, deer, the brook. These subjects he takes seriously; he has towards them "an earnest love that laid the swale in rows." But this is a continent that the pioneers have only recently conquered. The elemental spirits, which wish ill to man, are still lurking in the woods—to the imaginative poet. Through the activities of the countryside, in which people express themselves, Frost arrives at a homely philosophy close to the earth, wholesome, at times profound, and with the truth of generations behind it. He appears to have hit upon it, rather than searched for it. "The fact is the sweetest dream that labour knows." He wishes his epitaph to be, "I had a lover's quarrel with the world."

Understatement is the note he sounds most often. It lends irony to even a direct statement, which is said deprecatingly with a shrug or an apology as if to say, "This may be so, but don't take my word for it. It is just how I see it; others may see it differently. But this *is* one way of looking at it—and *I* like this way." This is the tone of the characteristic neighbourly New Englander, who is possessed of an innate simplicity and innocence and a natural wisdom, shrewd and earthy, which he voices laconically and in undertones, with a preference for whimsical and ironical understatement.

All Frost insists on is what he believes to find in all poets—absolute fidelity to the postures which the voice assumes in the most expressive intimate speech. . . . He has trusted his conviction that a man will not easily write better than he speaks when some matter has touched him deeply. . . . His poems are revolutionary because they lack the exaggeration of rhetoric. Many, if not most, of the separate lines and separate sentences are plain and in themselves nothing. But they are bound together and made elements of beauty by a calm eagerness of emotion.

EDWARD THOMAS

Mending Wall

Something there is that doesn't love a wall,
That sends the frozen-ground-swell under it,
And spills the upper boulders in the sun;
And makes gaps even two can pass abreast.
The work of hunters is another thing:
I have come after them and made repair
Where they have left not one stone on a stone,
But they would have the rabbit out of hiding,
To please the yelping dogs. The gaps I mean,
No one has seen them made or heard them made,　10
But at spring mending-time we find them there.
I let my neighbour know beyond the hill;
And on a day we meet to walk the line
And set the wall between us once again.
We keep the wall between us as we go.
To each the boulders that have fallen to each.
And some are loaves and some so nearly balls
We have to use a spell to make them balance:
"Stay where you are until our backs are turned!"
We wear our fingers rough with handling them.　20
Oh, just another kind of outdoor game,
One on a side. It comes to little more:
There where it is we do not need the wall:
He is all pine and I am apple orchard.
My apple trees will never get across
And eat the cones under his pines, I tell him.
He only says, "Good fences make good neighbours."
Spring is the mischief in me, and I wonder

If I could put a notion in his head:
'*Why* do they make good neighbours? Isn't it   30
Where there are cows? But here there are no cows.
Before I built a wall I'd ask to know
What I was walling in or walling out,
And to whom I was like to give offence.
Something there is that doesn't love a wall,
That wants it down.' I could say 'Elves' to him,
But it's not elves exactly, and I'd rather
He said it for himself. I see him there
Bringing a stone grasped firmly by the top
In each hand, like an old-stone savage armed.   40
He moves in darkness as it seems to me,
Not of woods only and the shade of trees.
He will not go behind his father's saying,
And he likes having thought of it so well
He says again, "Good fences make good neighbours."

Goodbye and keep Cold

This saying goodbye on the edge of the dark
And the cold to an orchard so young in the bark
Reminds me of all that can happen to harm
An orchard away at the end of the farm
All winter, cut off by a hill from the house.
I don't want it girdled by rabbit and mouse,
I don't want it dreamily nibbled for browse
By deer, and I don't want it budded by grouse.
(If certain it wouldn't be idle to call
I'd summon grouse, rabbit, and deer to the wall   10
And warn them away with a stick for a gun.)

I don't want it stirred by the heat of the sun.
(We made it secure against being, I hope,
By setting it out on a northerly slope.)
No orchard's the worse for the wintriest storm;
But one thing about it, it mustn't get warm.
'How often already you've had to be told,
Keep cold, young orchard. Goodbye and keep cold.
Dread fifty above more than fifty below.'
I have to be gone for a season or so.   20
My business awhile is with different trees,
Less carefully nurtured, less fruitful than these,
And such as is done to their wood with an axe—
Maples and birches and tamaracks.
I wish I could promise to lie in the night
And think of an orchard's arboreal plight
When slowly (and nobody comes with a light)
Its heart sinks lower under the sod.
But something has to be left to God.

Mowing

There was never a sound beside the wood but one,
And that was my long scythe whispering to the
        ground.
What was it it whispered? I knew not well myself;
Perhaps it was something about the heat of the sun,
Something, perhaps, about the lack of sound—
And that was why it whispered and did not speak.
It was no dream of the gift of idle hours,
Or easy gold at the hand of fay or elf:

Anything more than the truth would have seemed
    too weak
To the earnest love that laid the swale in rows,   10
Not without feeble-pointed spikes of flowers
(Pale orchises), and scared a bright green snake.
The fact is the sweetest dream that labour knows.
My long scythe whispered and left the hay to make.

After Apple-picking

My long two-pointed ladder's sticking through a tree
Toward heaven still,
And there's a barrel that I didn't fill
Beside it, and there may be two or three
Apples I didn't pick upon some bough.
But I am done with apple-picking now.
Essence of winter sleep is on the night,
The scent of apples: I am drowsing off.
I cannot rub the strangeness from my sight
I got from looking through a pane of glass   10
I skimmed this morning from the drinking trough
And held against the world of hoary grass.
It melted, and I let it fall and break.
But I was well
Upon my way to sleep before it fell,
And I could tell
What form my dreaming was about to take.
Magnified apples appear and disappear,
Stem end and blossom end,
And every fleck of russet showing clear.   20

My instep arch not only keeps the ache,
It keeps the pressure of a ladder-round.
I feel the ladder sway as the boughs bend.
And I keep hearing from the cellar bin
The rumbling sound
Of load on load of apples coming in.
For I have had too much
Of apple-picking: I am overtired
Of the great harvest I myself desired.
There were ten thousand thousand fruit to
     touch,   30
Cherish in hand, lift down, and not let fall.
For all
That struck the earth,
No matter if not bruised or spiked with stubble,
Went sure to the cider-apple heap
As of no worth.
One can see what will trouble
This sleep of mine, whatever sleep it is.
Were he not gone,
The woodchuck could say whether it's like his   40
Long sleep, as I describe its coming on,
Or just some human sleep.

Stopping by Woods on a Snowy Evening

Whose woods these are I think I know.
His house is in the village though;
He will not see me stopping here
To watch his woods fill up with snow.

My little horse must think it queer
To stop without a farmhouse near
Between the woods and frozen lake
The darkest evening of the year.

He gives his harness bells a shake
To ask if there is some mistake.   10
The only other sound's the sweep
Of easy wind and downy flake.

The woods are lovely, dark and deep,
But I have promises to keep,
And miles to go before I sleep,
And miles to go before I sleep.

Birches

When I see birches bend to left and right
Across the lines of straighter darker trees,
I like to think some boy's been swinging them.
But swinging doesn't bend them down to stay
As ice-storms do. Often you must have seen them
Loaded with ice a sunny winter morning
After a rain. They click upon themselves
As the breeze rises, and turn many-coloured
As the stir cracks and crazes their enamel.
Soon the sun's warmth makes them shed crystal   10
    shells
Shattering and avalanching on the snow-crust—
Such heaps of broken glass to sweep away
You'd think the inner dome of heaven had fallen.

They are dragged to the withered bracken by the
        load,
And they seem not to break; though once they are
        bowed
So low for long, they never right themselves:
You may see their trunks arching in the woods
Years afterwards, trailing their leaves on the ground
Like girls on hands and knees that throw their hair
Before them over their heads to dry in the sun.   20
But I was going to say when Truth broke in
With all her matter-of-fact about the ice-storm
I should prefer to have some boy bend them
As he went out and in to fetch the cows—
Some boy too far from town to learn baseball,
Whose only play was what he found himself,
Summer or winter, and could play alone.
One by one he subdued his father's trees
By riding them down over and over again
Until he took the stiffness out of them,   30
And not one but hung limp, not one was left
For him to conquer. He learned all there was
To learn about not launching out too soon
And so not carrying the tree away
Clear to the ground. He always kept his poise
To the top branches, climbing carefully
With the same pains you use to fill a cup
Up to the brim, and even above the brim.
Then he flung outward, feet first, with a swish,
Kicking his way down through the air to the
        ground.   40
So was I once myself a swinger of birches.
And so I dream of going back to be.

It's when I'm weary of considerations,
And life is too much like a pathless wood
Where your face burns and tickles with the cobwebs
Broken across it, and one eye is weeping
From a twig's having lashed across it open.
I'd like to get away from earth awhile
And then come back to it and begin over.
May no fate wilfully misunderstand me   50
And half grant what I wish and snatch me away
Not to return. Earth's the right place for love:
I don't know where it's likely to go better.
I'd like to go by climbing a birch tree,
And climb black branches up a snow-white trunk
Toward heaven, till the tree could bear no more,
But dipped its top and set me down again.
That would be good both going and coming back.
One could do worse than be a swinger of birches.

Ghost House

I dwell in a lonely house I know
That vanished many a summer ago,
    And left no trace but the cellar walls,
    And a cellar in which the daylight falls
And the purple-stemmed wild raspberries grow.

O'er ruined fences the grapevines shield
The woods come back to the mowing field;
    The orchard tree has grown one copse

Of new wood and old where the woodpecker
    chops;
The footpath down to the well is healed.   10

I dwell with a strangely aching heart
In that vanished abode there far apart
    On that disused and forgotten road
    That has no dust-bath now for the toad.
Night comes; the black bats tumble and dart;

The whippoorwill is coming to shout
And hush and cluck and flutter about:
    I hear him begin far enough away
    Full many a time to say his say
Before he arrives to say it out.   20

It is under the small, dim, summer star.
I know not who these mute folk are
    Who share the unlit place with me—
    Those stones out under the low-limbed tree
Doubtless bear names that the mosses mar.

They are tireless folk, but slow and sad,
Though two, close-keeping, are lass and lad,—
    With none among them that ever sings,
    And yet, in view of how many things,
As sweet companions as might be had.   30

Into my Own

One of my wishes is that those dark trees,
So old and firm they scarcely show the breeze,
Were not, as 'twere, the merest mask of gloom,
But stretched away unto the edge of doom.

I should not be withheld but that some day
Into their vastness I should steal away,
Fearless of ever finding open land,
Or highway where the slow wheel pours the sand.

I do not see why I should e'er turn back,
Or those should not set forth upon my track   10
To overtake me, who should miss me here
And long to know if still I held them dear.

They would not find me changed from him they
          knew—
Only more sure of all I thought was true.

Two look at Two

Love and forgetting might have carried them
A little further up the mountainside
With night so near, but not much further up.
They must have halted soon in any case
With thoughts of the path back, how rough it was
With rock and washout, and unsafe in darkness;

When they were halted by a tumbled wall
With barbed-wire binding. They stood facing this,
Spending what onward impulse they still had
In one last look the way they must not go,   10
On up the failing path, if a stone
Or earthslide moved at night, it moved itself;
No footstep moved it. "This is all," they sighed,
"Good-night to woods." But not so; there was
    more.
A doe from round a spruce stood looking at them
Across the wall, as near the wall as they.
She saw them in their field, they her in hers.
The difficulty of seeing what stood still,
Like some up-ended boulder split in two,
Was in her clouded eyes: they saw no fear there.   20
She seemed to think that two thus they were safe.
Then, as if they were something that, though strange,
She could not trouble her mind with too long,
She sighed and passed unscared along the wall.
"This, then, is all. What more is there to ask?"
But no, not yet. A snort to bid them wait.
A buck from round the spruce stood looking at them
Across the wall as near the wall as they.
This was an antlered buck of lusty nostril,
Not the same doe come back into her place.   30
He viewed them quizzically with jerks of head,
As if to ask, 'Why don't you make some motion?
Or give some sign of life? Because you can't.
I doubt if you're as living as you look.'
Thus till he had them almost feeling dared
To stretch a proffering hand—and a spell-breaking.
Then he too passed unscared along the wall.

Two had seen two, whichever side you spoke from.
'This *must* be all.' It was all. Still they stood,
A great wave from it going over them,   40
As if the earth in one unlooked-for favour
Had made them certain earth returned their love.

THOMAS HARDY (1840–1928)
O.M., 1910.

Born near Dorchester. Apprenticed to an ecclesiastical architect. Gave up architecture for literature. He was a poet before he was a novelist, and in his twenties "practised the writing of poetry very assiduously," but abandoned that art when he began his career as a novelist. In all his work Nature forms a background to, if not a cause of, man's conflict and tragedy. Works include: *Desperate Remedies* (1871); *The Return of the Native* (1878); *The Mayor of Casterbridge* (1886); *Wessex Poems* (1898); *Time's Laughing-Stocks* (1909); *The Dynasts* (1908)—an epic-drama; *Late Lyrics and Earlier* (1922); *Winter Words* (1928); *Collected Poems* (1928).

When in 1895 Hardy was shocked and sickened by the reception of his latest novel, *Jude the Obscure*, he was confirmed in his determination to write no more novels (having written all the novels he wished to write) and to write only poetry. Poetry had been his first love and it was to be his medium of expression for the remaining thirty years of his life. No other English writer has equalled Hardy's achievement as both novelist and poet.

Born and bred a Dorset man and living most of his life in Dorchester, Hardy was closer to the English peasantry than any other poet since Langland. His education, superior to that of most country people, enabled him, while sharing the exact and detailed knowledge and the intimate feelings of his fellow countrymen, to stand detached from them and to see in their actions a depth and a significance that they could not perceive. The town was fast encroaching on the country, and none saw more clearly than Hardy what the growing advance of industrialism would do to the country and countrymen and what the new belief in scientific evolution would do to old beliefs. Against this background of change and uncertainty Hardy found his subjects in the circumstances of everyday life—for example, lovers parting by a street lamp—and he transformed them into poetry while keeping their reality and their contact with common life. The poetry lay in the situation, and this situation came from his own life, the life of others, nature, history, folk-lore. In each situation he chose the crucial moment of conflict or crisis to which the whole of the previous existence of the beings had been moving.

In these circumstances, as in all else, Man is not the master of his destiny; he is the slave of what Hardy calls "The Immanent Will":

> In the Foretime, even to the germ of Being,
> Nothing appears of shape to indicate
> That cognizance has marshalled things terrene,
> Or will (such is my thinking) in my span.
> Rather they show that, like a knitter drowsed,
> Whose fingers play in skilled unmindfulness,
> The Will has woven with an absent heed
> Since life first was; and ever will so weave.

The Dynasts

With a poet's unerring instinct for a title Hardy summed up much of his view of life in the titles of four of his volumes of verse: *Satires of Circumstance; Life's Little Ironies; Time's Laughing-Stocks;* and *Moments of Vision.* Nature is indifferent to human values; Chance is blind; Time is cruel and insatiable. But, because he cannot control his own destiny, man is to be admired the more for the courage and fortitude with which he faces the inevitable, and to be praised the more for the barriers, useless though they ultimately are, that he erects against Fate and "crass casualty"—love and comradeship, generosity and self-sacrifice, beauty and joy, the desire for perfection where nothing is perfect, delight in simple things—dances, church-music, the weather, dogs, bird-song, first love. It is Hardy's refusal to burke the issue, to turn his back on the inevitable, that makes him a great poet. It is not pessimism, for it faces the truth, the reality, and, seeing it for what it is, paints it in its true colours. In its various incidents life plays many tricks on one, but one must face its ironies uncompromisingly and with an equal irony. The dying husband overhears his wife ordering widow's clothes which must be "of latest fashion." Such is the satire of circumstance, seen in life's many chances and changes, all of which Hardy knows intimately. Many of his poems seize such an odd moment in man's good or evil fortune, and draw universal significance from this one moment. That is one of the greatest powers of the great poet. "The real function of poetry is the application of ideas to life, in Arnold's phrase, and my own contains such an application." (Hardy: Preface to *Late Lyrics and Earlier*.)

Hardy's language has the simplicity of a countryman's speech coupled with the sophisticated vocabulary of an educated man. Such a mixture sounds as if it would not blend. But in Hardy's hands it does blend and has an individual and idiosyncratic tang, which perfectly fits the shape of the thought, just as his rhythm, in the simple yet varied stanza-form, echoes the feeling. Country words, close to everyday things, mingle with pedantic and resonant Latinisms and obsolete and earthy Anglo-Saxon words, and the result has a unique effect that only Hardy has achieved. Sometimes the combination has the clumsiness of prose and falls short of the aim, but more often it triumphantly succeeds. While the country phrase makes the experience and the reaction to it close and familiar and convinces us of its authenticity, the more formal phrase detaches Hardy from the experience and gives it weight, depth, and universality.

Drummer Hodge

They throw in Drummer Hodge, to rest
    Uncoffined—just as found:
His landmark is a kopje-crest
    That breaks the veldt around;
And foreign constellations west
    Each night above his mound.

Young Hodge the Drummer never knew—
    Fresh from his Wessex home—
The meaning of the broad Karoo,
    The Bush, the dusty loam,
And why uprose to nightly view
    Strange stars amid the gloam.

Yet portion of that unknown plain
    Will Hodge for ever be;
His homely Northern breast and brain
    Grow to some Southern tree,
And strange-eyed constellations reign
    His stars eternally.

The Darkling Thrush

I leant upon a coppice gate
    When Frost was spectre-gray,
And Winter's dregs made desolate
    The weakening eye of day.

The tangled bine-stems scored the sky
    Like strings of broken lyres,
And all mankind that haunted nigh
    Had sought their household fires.

The land's sharp features seemed to be
    The Century's corpse outleant,   10
His crypt the cloudy canopy,
    The wind his death-lament.
The ancient pulse of germ and birth
    Was shrunken hard and dry,
And every spirit upon earth
    Seemed fervourless as I.

At once a voice arose among
    The bleak twigs overhead
In a full-hearted evensong
    Of joy illimited;   20
An aged thrush, frail, gaunt, and small,
    In blast-beruffled plume,
Had chosen thus to fling his soul
    Upon the growing gloom.

So little cause for carolings
    Of such ecstatic sound
Was written on terrestrial things
    Afar or nigh around,
That I could think there trembled through
    His happy good-night air   30
Some blessed Hope, whereof he knew
    And I was unaware.

In Time of "The Breaking of Nations"

Only a man harrowing clods
    In a slow silent walk
With an old horse that stumbles and nods
    Half asleep as they stalk.

Only thin smoke without flame
    From the heaps of couch-grass;
Yet this will go onward the same
    Though Dynasties pass.

Yonder a maid and her wight
    Come whispering by: 10
War's annals will cloud into night
    Ere their story die.

Friends Beyond

William Dewy, Tranter Reuben, Farmer Ledlow late
    at plough,
    Robert's kin, and John's, and Ned's,
And the Squire, and Lady Susan, lie in Mellstock
    churchyard now!

"Gone," I call them, gone for good, that group of
    local hearts and heads;
    Yet at mothy curfew-tide,
And at midnight when the noon-heat breathes it back
    from walls and leads,

They've a way of whispering to me—fellow-wight
        who yet abide—
  In the muted, measured note
Of a ripple under archways, or a lone cave's stillicide:

" We have triumphed: this achievement turns the bane
        to antidote,   10
  Unsuccesses to success,
Many thought-worn eves and morrows to a morrow
        free of thought.

"No more need we corn and clothing, feel of old
        terrestial stress:
  Chill detraction stirs no sigh;
Fear of death has even bygone us: death gave all that
        we possess."

W.D.—"Ye mid burn the old bass-viol that I set such
        value by."
Squire—"You may hold the manse in fee,
  You may wed my spouse, may let my children's
        memory of me die."

Lady S.—"You may have my rich brocades, my laces;
        take each household key;
  Ransack coffer, desk, bureau: 20
Quiz the few poor treasures hid there, con the
        letters kept by me."

Far.—"Ye mid zell my favourite heifer, ye mid let the
        charlock grow,
  Foul the grinterns, give up thrift."

Far. Wife—"If ye break my best blue china, children,
      I shan't care or ho."

All—"We've no wish to hear the tidings, how the
          people's fortunes shift;
      What your daily doings are;
      Who are wedded, born, divided; if your lives beat
          slow or swift.

"Curious not the least are we if our intents you make
          or mar,
      If you quire to our old tune,
If the City stage still passes, if the weirs still roar
          afar."   30

—Thus, with very gods' composure, freed those
          crosses late and soon
      Which, in life, the Trine allow
(Why, none witteth), and ignoring all that haps
          beneath the moon,

William Dewy, Tranter Reuben, Farmer Ledlow late
          at plough,
      Robert's kin, and John's, and Ned's,
And the Squire, and Lady Susan, murmur mildly to
      me now.

Afterwards

When the Present has latched its postern behind my
                tremulous stay,
    And the May month flaps its glad green leaves like
                wings,
Delicate-filmed as new-spun silk, will the neighbours
        say,
    "He was a man who used to notice such things"?

If it be in the dusk when, like an eyelid's soundless
        blink,
    The dewfall-hawk comes crossing the shades to
        alight
Upon the wind-warped upland thorn, a gazer may
        think,
    "To him this must have been a familiar sight."

If I pass during some nocturnal blackness, mothy and
        warm,
    When the hedgehog travels furtively over the
        lawn,   10
One may say, "He strove that such innocent creatures
        should come to no harm,
    But he could do little for them; and now he is
        gone."

If, when hearing that I have been stilled at last, they
        stand at the door,
    Watching the full-starred heavens that winter sees,

Will this thought rise on those who will meet my face
      no more,
  "He was one who had an eye for such mysteries"?

And will any say when my bell of quittance is heard in
      the gloom,
  And a crossing breeze cuts a pause in its out-
      rollings,
Till they rise again, as they were a new bell's boom,
  "He hears it not now, but used to notice such
      things"?   20

The Choirmaster's Burial

He often would ask us
That, when he died,
After playing so many
To their last rest,
If out of us any
Should here abide,
And it would not task us,
We would with our lutes
Play over him
By his grave-brim   10
The psalm he liked best—
The one whose sense suits
"Mount Ephraim"—
And perhaps we should seem
To him, in Death's dream,
Like the seraphim.

As soon as I knew
That his spirit was gone
I thought this his due,
And spoke thereupon.   20
"I think," said the vicar,
"A read service quicker
Than viols out-of-doors
In these frosts and hoars.
That old-fashioned way
Requires a fine day,
And it seems to me
It had better not be."

Hence, that afternoon,
Though never knew he   30
That his wish could not be,
To get through it faster
They buried the master
Without any tune.

But 'twas said that, when
At the dead of next night
The vicar looked out,
There struck on his ken
Thronged roundabout,
Where the frost was graying   40
The headstoned grass,
A band all in white
Like the saints in church-glass,
Singing and playing
The ancient stave
By the choirmaster's grave.

Such the tenor man told
When he had grown old.

An August Midnight

A shaded lamp and a waving blind,
And the beat of a clock from a distant floor:
On this scene enter—winged, horned, and spined—
A longlegs, a moth, and a dumbledore;
While 'mid my page there idly stands
A sleepy fly, that rubs its hands . . .

Thus meet we five, in this still place,
At this point of time, at this point in space.
—My guests besmear my new-penned line,
Or bang at the lamp and fall supine.   10
"God's humblest, they!" I muse. Yet why?
They know Earth-secrets that know not I.

The Moth-signal
(On Egdon Heath)

"What are you still, still thinking,"
    He asked in vague surmise,
"That you stare at the wick unblinking
    With those deep lost luminous eyes?"

"O, I see a poor moth burning
    In the candle flame," said she.
"Its wings and legs are turning
    To a cinder rapidly."

"Moths fly in from the heather,"
 He said, "now the days decline."   10
"I know," said she. "The weather,
 I hope, will at last be fine.

"I think," she added lightly,
 "I'll look out at the door.
The ring the moon wears nightly
 May be visible now no more."

She rose, and, little heeding,
 Her life-mate then went on
With his mute and museful reading
 In the annals of ages gone.   20

Outside the house a figure
 Came from the tumulus near,
And speedily waxed bigger,
 And clasped and called her Dear.

"I saw the pale-winged token
 You sent through the crack," sighed she.
"That moth is burnt and broken
 With which you lured out me.

"And were I as the moth is
 It might be better far   30
For one whose marriage troth is
 Shattered as potsherds are!"

Then grinned the Ancient Briton
    From the tumulus treed with pine:
"So, hearts are thwartly smitten
    In these days as in mine!"

At Middle-field Gate in February

The bars are thick with drops that show
    As they gather themselves from the fog
Like silver buttons ranged in a row,
And as evenly spaced as if measured, although
    They fall at the feeblest jog.

They load the leafless hedge hard by,
    And the blades of last year's grass.
While the fallow ploughland turned up nigh
In raw rolls, clammy and clogging lie—
    Too clogging for feet to pass.   10

How dry it was on a far-back day
    When straws hung the hedge and around,
When amid the sheaves in amorous play
In curtained bonnets and light array
    Bloomed a bevy now underground!

Beyond the Last Lamp
(Near Tooting Common)

While rain, with eve in partnership,
Descended darkly, drip, drip, drip,
Beyond the last lone lamp I passed

Walking slowly, whispering sadly,
   Two linked loiterers, wan, downcast:
Some heavy thought constrained each face,
And blinded them to time and place.

The pair seemed lovers, yet absorbed
In mental scenes no longer orbed
By love's young rays. Each countenance   10
   As it slowly, as it sadly
   Caught the lamplight's yellow glance,
Held in suspense a misery
At things which had been or might be.

When I retrod that watery way
Some hours beyond the droop of day,
Still I found pacing there the twain
   Just as slowly, just as sadly,
   Heedless of the night and rain.
One could but wonder who they were   20
And what wild woe detained them there.

Though thirty years of blur and blot
Have slid since I beheld that spot,
And saw in curious converse there
   Moving slowly, moving sadly
   That mysterious tragic pair,
Its olden look may linger on—
All but the couple; they have gone.

Whither? Who knows, indeed. . . . And yet
To me, when nights are weird and wet,
Without those comrades there at tryst   30

Creeping slowly, creeping sadly,
That lone lane does not exist.
There they seem brooding on their pain,
And will, while such a lane remain.

The Voice

Woman much missed, how you call to me, call to me,
Saying that now you are not as you were
When you had changed from the one who was all to
me,
But as at first, when our day was fair.

Can it be you that I hear? Let me view you, then,
Standing as when I drew near to the town
Where you would wait for me: yes, as I knew you
then,
Even to the original air-blue gown!

Or is it only the breeze, in its listlessness
Travelling across the wet mead to me here,   10
You being ever dissolved to wan wistlessness,
Heard no more again far or near?

Thus I; faltering forward,
Leaves around me falling,
Wind oozing thin through the thorn from norward,
And the woman calling.

After a Journey

Hereto I come to view a voiceless ghost;
 Whither, O whither will its whim now draw me?
Up the cliff, down, till I'm lonely, lost,
 And the unseen waters' ejaculations awe me.
Where you will next be there's no knowing,
 Facing round about me everywhere,
   With your nut-coloured hair,
And gray eyes, and rose-flush coming and going.

Yes: I have re-entered your olden haunts at last;
 Through the years, through the dead scenes I have
   tracked you;   10
What have you now found to say of our past—
 Scanned across the dark space wherein I have
   lacked you?
Summer gave us sweets, but autumn wrought division?
 Things were not lastly as firstly well
   With us twain, you tell?
But all's closed now, despite Time's derision.

I see what you are doing: you are leading me on
 To the spots we knew when we haunted here
   together,
The waterfall, above which the mist-bow shone
 At the then fair hour in the then fair weather,   20
And the cave just under, with a voice still so hollow
 That it seems to call out to me from forty years ago,
   When you were all aglow,
And not the thin ghost that I now fraily follow!

Ignorant of what there is flitting here to see,
    The waked birds preen and the seals flop lazily;
Soon you will have, Dear, to vanish from me,
    For the stars close their shutters and the dawn
        whitens hazily.
Trust me, I mind not, though Life lours,
    The bringing me here; nay, bring me here again!
        I am just the same as when   30
Our days were a joy, and our paths through flowers.

At Castle Boterel

As I drive to the junction of lane and highway,
    And the drizzle bedrenches the waggonette,
I look behind at the fading byway,
    And see on its slope, now glistening wet,
        Distinctly yet

Myself and a girlish form benighted
    In dry March weather. We climb the road
Beside a chaise. We had just alighted
    To ease the sturdy pony's load
        When he sighed and slowed.   10

What we did as we climbed, and what we talked of
    Matters not much, nor to what it led,—
Something that life will not be balked of
    Without rude reason till hope is dead,
        And feeling fled.

It filled but a minute. But was there ever
   A time of such quality, since or before,
In that hill's story? To one mind never,
      Though it has been climbed, foot-swift, foot-sore,
         By thousands more.   20

Primaeval rocks form the road's steep border,
   And much have they faced there, first and last,
Of the transitory in Earth's long order;
      But what they record in colour and cast
         Is—that we two passed.

And to me, though Time's unflinching rigour,
   In mindless rote, has ruled from sight
The substance now, one phantom figure
      Remains on the slope, as when that night
         Saw us alight.   30

I look and see it there, shrinking, shrinking,
   I look back at it amid the rain
For the very last time; for my sand is sinking,
      And I shall traverse old love's domain
         Never again.

During Wind and Rain

   They sing their dearest songs—
   He, she, all of them—yea,
   Treble and tenor and bass,
      And one to play;
   With the candles mooning each face. . . .
      Ah, no; the years O!
How the sick leaves reel down in throngs!

They clear the creeping moss—
Elders and juniors—aye,
Making the pathways neat   10
   And the garden gay;
And they build a shady seat. . . .
    Ah, no; the years, the years;
See, the white storm-birds wing across.

They are blithely breakfasting all—
Men and maidens—yea,
Under the summer tree,
   With a glimpse of the bay,
While pet fowl come to the knee. . . .
    Ah, no; the years O!   20
And the rotten rose is ript from the wall.

They change to a high new house,
He, she, all of them—aye,
Clocks and carpets and chairs
   On the lawn all day,
And brightest things that are theirs. . . .
    Ah, no; the years, the years;
Down their carved names the rain-drop ploughs.

EDWIN MUIR (1887–1959)

Born at Deerness, Orkney Is. Educated Kirkwall
Burgh School, Orkney. After work in ship-building
offices on the Clyde, became journalist, translator, and
author. Assistant Editor of *The New Age*, 1919–21.
Co-editor of the *European Quarterly* since 1934. Warden
of Newbattle Abbey College, 1950–5. Works include:
The Marionette (1927), *The Three Brothers* (1931) and
Poor Tom (1932)—fiction; *First Poems* (1925); *Chorus
of the Newly-dead* (1926); *Transition* (1926) and *The Struc-
ture of the Novel* (1928)—criticism; *John Knox* (1929)—
biography; *Variations on a Time-theme* (1934); *Scottish
Journey* (1935)—travel; *Journeys and Places* (1937); *The
Present Age from 1914* (1939)—(Introductions to
English Literature Series); *The Narrow Place* (1943);
The Voyage (1946); *Essays on Literature and Society*
(1949); *The Labyrinth* (1949); *Collected Poems* (1952);
An Autobiography (1954) (revised and enlarged; first
published 1940); *One Foot in Eden* (1956).

The primitive facts, the eternal verities, of human
existence in the world engage the poet's mind. Love,
time, death, hope, faith, liberty, innocence, are the
subjects of Edwin Muir's poetry, all seen with inte-
grity of mind and a clear-sighted love of the truth.

The main theme of Muir's poetry is the conflict
between Time and Eternity. His poems express his
varying thoughts about Time's reality, and attempt to
solve this opposition of Time and Eternity. Time is
seen from many angles and in many ages; each poem
presents one aspect of Time in one place, the whole
making a coherent picture. Man is the slave of Time,

but Time is also the agent of Eternity. Time is the destroyer of beauty, but Time is also a creator. Time is an unbreakable chain of events, but it may lead from Eden, the world before the Fall, the age of Blake's 'Innocence,' through the labyrinth to a future destination of hope and contentment. Against the Greek conception of 'fixed Fate' and inevitable Destiny stands the Christian faith of the Resurrection with its hope of salvation.

Much in Muir's character and outlook has been determined by his upbringing in the Orkneys, "the difficult land." He feels strongly the racial forces of Scotland and is moved deeply by the hardy fortitude and noble perseverance of his race, as, in the face of privation, it strives to wrest a living from a difficult and unproductive soil.

"The Orkney I was born into," says Muir, "was a place where there was no great distinction between the ordinary and the fabulous; the lives of living men turned into legend." For Muir these two worlds, of the real and the fabulous, fuse and are one. He is as much at home in one as in the other, and both are described with equal realism and concreteness, the image for either often being derived from the landscape of the Orkneys and the memories of his childhood there. One of his most striking qualities derives from this fusion: his power of translating a myth, an abstract theme of conflict or endeavour, into concrete imagery and language, for example *The Combat*. "In themselves," he writes, "our conscious lives may not be particularly interesting. But what we are not and can never be, our fable, seems to me inconceivably interesting." Hence, his autobiography is entitled *The Story and the Fable*.

The Combat

It was not meant for human eyes,
That combat on the shabby patch
Of clods and trampled turf that lies
Somewhere beneath the sodden skies
For eye of toad or adder to catch.

And having seen it I accuse
The crested animal in his pride,
Arrayed in all the royal hues
Which hide the claws he well can use
To tear the heart out of the side.   10

Body of leopard, eagle's head
And whetted beak, and lion's mane,
And frost-grey hedge of feathers spread
Behind—he seemed of all things bred.
I shall not see his like again.

As for his enemy, there came in
A soft round beast as brown as clay;
All rent and patched his wretched skin;
A battered bag he might have been,
Some old used thing to throw away.   20

Yet he awaited face to face
The furious beast and the swift attack.
Soon over and done. That was no place
Or time for chivalry or for grace.
The fury had him on his back.

And two small paws like hands flew out
To right and left as the trees stood by.
One would have said beyond a doubt
This was the very end of the bout,
But that the creature would not die.   30

For ere the death-stroke he was gone,
Writhed, whirled, huddled into his den,
Safe somehow there. The fight was done,
And he had lost who had all but won.
But oh his deadly fury then.

A while the place lay blank, forlorn,
Drowsing as in relief from pain.
The cricket chirped, the grating thorn
Stirred, and a little sound was born.
The champions took their posts again.   40

And all began. The stealthy paw
Slashed out and in. Could nothing save
These rags and tatters from the claw?
Nothing. And yet I never saw
A beast so helpless and so brave.

And now, while the trees stand watching, still
The unequal battle rages there,
And the killing beast that cannot kill
Swells and swells in his fury till
You'd almost think it was despair.   50

The Confirmation

Yes, yours, my love, is the right human face.
I in my mind had waited for this long,
Seeing the false and searching for the true,
Then found you as a traveller finds a place
Of welcome suddenly amid the wrong
Valleys and rocks and twisting roads. But you,
What shall I call you? A fountain in a waste,
A well of water in a country dry,
Or anything that's honest and good, an eye
That makes the whole world bright. Your open
       heart,   10
Simple with giving, gives the primal deed,
The first good world, the blossom, the blowing seed,
The hearth, the steadfast land, the wandering sea,
Not beautiful or rare in every part,
But like yourself, as they were meant to be.

Horses

Those lumbering horses in the steady plough,
On the bare field—I wonder why, just now,
They seemed terrible, so wild and strange,
Like magic power on the stony grange.

Perhaps some childish hour has come again,
When I watched fearful, through the blackening rain,
Their hooves like pistons in an ancient mill
Move up and down, yet seem as standing still.

Their conquering hooves which trod the stubble
    down
Were ritual that turned the fields to brown,   10
And their great hulks were seraphim of gold
Or mute ecstatic monsters on the mould.

And oh the rapture, when, one furrow done,
They marched broad-breasted to the sinking sun!
The light flowed off their bossy sides in flakes;
The furrows rolled behind like struggling snakes.

But when at dusk with steaming nostrils home
They came, they seemed gigantic in the gloam,
And warm and glowing with mysterious fire
That lit their smouldering bodies in the mire.   20

Their eyes as brilliant and as wide as night
Gleamed with a cruel apocalyptic light.
Their manes the leaping ire of the wind
Lifted with rage invisible and blind.

Ah, now it fades! it fades! and I must pine
Again for that dread country crystalline,
Where the blank field and the still-standing tree
Were bright and fearful presences to me.

The Difficult Land

This is a difficult land. Here things miscarry
Whether we care, or do not care enough.
The grain may pine, the harlot weed grow haughty,
Sun, rain and frost alike conspire against us:

You'd think there was malice in the very air.
And the spring floods and summer droughts: our
    fields
Mile after mile of soft and useless dust.
On dull delusive days presaging rain
We yoke the oxen, go out harrowing,
Walk in the middle of an ochre cloud,   10
Dust rising before us and falling again behind us,
Slowly and gently settling where it lay.
These days the earth itself looks sad and senseless.
And when next day the sun mounts hot and lusty
We shake our fists and kick the ground in anger.
We have strange dreams: as that, in the early morning
We stand and watch the silver drift of stars
Turn suddenly to a flock of black-birds flying.
And once in a lifetime men from over the border,
In early summer, the season of fresh campaigns,   20
Come trampling down the corn, and kill our cattle.
These things we know and by good luck or guidance
Either frustrate or, if we must, endure.
We are a people; race and speech support us,
Ancestral rite and custom, roof and tree,
Our songs that tell of our triumphs and disasters
(Fleeting alike), continuance of fold and hearth,
Our names and callings, work and rest and sleep,
And something that, defeated, still endures—
These things sustain us. Yet there are times   30
When name, identity, and our very hands,
Senselessly labouring, grow most hateful to us,
And we would gladly rid us of these burdens
(Which yet are knit to us as flesh to bone),
Enter our darkness through the doors of wheat

And the light veil of grass (leaving behind
Name, body, country, speech, vocation, faith)
And gather into the secrecy of the earth
Furrowed by broken ploughs lost deep in time.

We have such hours, but are drawn back again   40
By faces of goodness, faithful masks of sorrow,
Honesty, kindness, courage, fidelity,
The love that lasts a life's time. And the fields,
Homestead and stall and barn, springtime and
        autumn.

(For we can love even the wandering seasons
In their inhuman circuit.) And the dead
Who lodge in us so strangely, unremembered,
Yet in their place. For how can we reject
The long last look on the ever-dying face
Turned backward from the other side of time?   50
And how offend the dead and shame the living
By these despairs? And how refrain from love?
This is a difficult country, and our home.

The Child Dying

Unfriendly friendly universe,
I pack your stars into my purse,
And bid you, bid you so farewell,
That I can leave you, quite go out,
Go out, go out beyond all doubt,
My father says, is the miracle.

You are so great, and I so small:
I am nothing, you are all:
Being nothing, I can take this way.
Oh, I need neither rise nor fall,   10
For when I do not move at all
I shall be out of all your day.

It's said some memory will remain
In the other place, grass in the rain,
Light on the land, sun on the sea,
A flitting grace, a phantom face,
But the world is out. There is no place
Where it and its ghost can ever be.

Father, father, I dread this air
Blown from the far side of despair,   20
The cold cold corner. What house, what hold,
What hand is there? I look and see
Nothing-filled eternity,
And the great round world grows weak and old.

Hold my hand, oh hold it fast—
I am changing!—until at last
My hand in yours no more will change,
Though yours change on. You here, I there,
So hand in hand, twin-leafed despair—
I did not know death was so strange.   30

The Horses

Barely a twelvemonth after
The seven days war that put the world to sleep,
Late in the evening the strange horses came.
By then we had made our covenant with silence,
But in the first few days it was so still
We listened to our breathing and were afraid.
On the second day
The radios failed; we turned the knobs; no answer.
On the third day a warship passed us, heading north,
Dead bodies piled on the deck. On the sixth day   10
A plane plunged over us into the sea. Thereafter
Nothing. The radios dumb;
And still they stand in corners of our kitchens,
And stand, perhaps, turned on, in a million rooms
All over the world. But now if they should speak,
If on a sudden they should speak again,
If on the stroke of noon a voice should speak,
We would not listen, we would not let it bring
That old bad world that swallowed its children quick
At one great gulp. We would not have it again.   20
Sometimes we think of the nations lying asleep,
Curled blindly in impenetrable sorrow,
And then the thought confounds us with its
        strangeness.

The tractors lie about our fields; at evening
They look like dank sea-monsters couched and
        waiting.
We leave them where they are and let them rust:

'They'll moulder away and be like other loam'.
We make our oxen drag our rusty ploughs,
Long laid aside. We have gone back
Far past our fathers' land.
                  And then, that evening   30
Late in the summer the strange horses came.
We heard a distant tapping on the road,
A deepening drumming; it stopped, went on again,
And at the corner changed to hollow thunder.
We saw the heads
Like a wild wave charging and were afraid.
We had sold our horses in our fathers' time
To buy new tractors. Now they were strange to us
As fabulous steeds set on an ancient shield
Or illustrations in a book of knights.   40
We did not dare go near them. Yet they waited,
Stubborn and shy, as if they had been sent
By an old command to find our whereabouts
And that long-lost archaic companionship.
In the first moment we had never a thought
That they were creatures to be owned and used.
Among them were some half-a-dozen colts
Dropped in some wilderness of the broken world,
Yet new as if they had come from their own Eden.
Since then they have pulled our ploughs and borne
     our loads,   50
But that free servitude still can pierce our hearts.
Our life is changed; their coming our beginning.

Into thirty centuries born

Into thirty centuries born,
At home in them all but the very last,
We meet ourselves at every turn
In the long country of the past.
There the fallen are up again
In mortality's second day,
There the indisputable dead
Rise in flesh more fine than clay
And the dead selves we cast away
In imperfection are perfected,   10
And all is plain yet never found out!
Ilium burns before our eyes
For thirty centuries never put out,
And we walk the streets of Troy
And breathe in the air its fabulous name.
The king, the courtier and the rout
Shall never perish in that flame;
Old Priam shall become a boy
For ever changed, for ever the same.
What various sights these countries show: 20
The horses on the roundabout
Still flying round the glittering ring
That rusted fifty years ago.
The gunboat in the little bay,
A mile, and half an age away.
Methuselah letting the years go by
While death was new and still in doubt
And only a dream the thought, 'To die.'
And round a corner you may see

Man, maid and tempter under the tree: 30
You'd think there was no sense in death.
And nothing to remedy, nothing to blame;
The dark Enchanter is your friend.
Is it fantasy or faith
That keeps intact that marvellous show
And saves the helpless dead from harm?—
To-morrow sounds the great alarm
That puts the histories to rout;
To-morrow and to-morrow brings
Endless beginning without end.   40

Then on this moment set your foot,
Take your road for everywhere,
And from your roving barrier shoot
Your arrow into the empty air.
Follow at a careful pace,
Else you may wander in despair.
Gathered at your moving post
Is all that you have but memory.
This is the place of hope and fear,
And faith that comes when hope is lost.   50
Defeat and victory both are here.
In this place where all's to be,
In this moment you are free,
And bound to all. For you shall know
Before you Troy goes up in fire,
And you shall walk the Trojan streets
When home are sailed the murdering fleets,
Priam shall be a little boy,
Time shall cancel time's deceits,

And you shall weep for grief and joy 60
To see the whole world perishing
Into everlasting spring,
And over and over the opening briar.

EDWARD THOMAS (1878–1917)

Educated St Paul's School and Lincoln College, Oxford. Killed in action, April 1917. Works include: *The Woodland Life* (1897)—nature studies; *Horæ Solitariæ* (1902); *The Heart of England* (1909); *The South Country* (1909); *Life of Richard Jefferies* (1909); *Borrow* (1912); *Four and Twenty Blackbirds* (1915)—short stories; *Poems* (1917); *The Last Sheaf* (1928)—prose fragments; *The Childhood of Edward Thomas* (1938)—a fragment of autobiography.

The countryside of England was the main theme of Edward Thomas's poetry. This countryside he knew intimately and lovingly, with a countryman's knowledge and affection. He was genuinely a Nature poet: he felt instinctively those emotions that Nature can inspire, and he transmitted them directly to his reader in a conversational diction and rhythm that he developed from Robert Frost's. For him Nature had that power of consolation that Wordsworth found in it. The simplest and commonest sights and sounds of the countryside gave him happiness and a feeling of the beauty that lies beyond them. Hesitantly, diffidently, he discovered the life of the creatures of Nature and groped towards the greater life of which they are symbols and manifestations, uncovering on the way some moral or spiritual truth—as with Robert Frost, never the object of his poem but a by-product of it. He felt that all creatures of Nature and all growing things have a life in common, and that man also shares this life. In the discovery of Nature he found himself;

in learning how to look at Nature, he also learnt how to look at himself.

Quick observation, based on sympathy, started off many of the poems. Although, like Keats, he was aware of the transience of all beautiful things, also like Keats he knew that verse can give permanence to this beauty. His refusal to ignore the more cruel aspects of Nature, his acceptance of the difference between things as they are and things as they might be, in other words his honesty, pervades his work. His absolute sincerity is found in his poems as in his dealings with people; it is in keeping with his character. He was shy, reserved, reticent, and contemplative, but with great personal charm and an honesty that could be ruthless. He had a sense of humour, was sympathetic to suffering, was loyal and kind and sensitive, had a deep self-distrust and melancholia, and had a deep capacity of joy in beauty.

In *Edward Thomas: the Last Four Years*, Eleanor Farjeon says of the poet that "in all his thirty-nine years he kept his senses fresh, and liked what he saw. He saw more than anybody else, and he saw it day and night. The seasons and the weather never failed him. . . . Of his poem *Aspens*, he said, '*I* was the aspen. 'We' meant the trees and I with my dejected shyness.'"

The Manor Farm

The rock-like mud unfroze a little and rills
Ran and sparkled down each side of the road
Under the catkins wagging in the hedge.
But earth would have her sleep out, spite of the sun;
Nor did I value that thin gilding beam
More than a pretty February thing
Till I came down to the old Manor Farm,
And church and yew-tree opposite, in age
Its equals and in size. The church and yew
And farmhouse slept in a Sunday silentness.   10
The air raised not a straw. The steep farm roof,
With tiles duskily glowing, entertained
The mid-day sun; and up and down the roof
White pigeons nestled. There was no sound but one.
Three cart-horses were looking over a gate
Drowsily through their forelocks, swishing their
        tails
Against a fly, a solitary fly.

The Winter's cheek flushed as if he had drained
Spring, Summer, and Autumn at a draught
And smiled quietly. But 'twas not Winter—   20
Rather a season of bliss unchangeable
Awakened from farm and church where it had lain
Safe under tile and thatch for ages since
This England, Old already, was called Merry.

Swedes

They have taken the gable from the roof of clay
On the long swede pile. They have let in the sun
To the white and gold and purple of curled fronds
Unsunned. It is a sight more tender-gorgeous
At the wood-corner where Winter moans and drips
Than when, in the Valley of the Tombs of Kings,
A boy crawls down into a Pharaoh's tomb
And, first of Christian men, beholds the mummy,
God and monkey, chariot and throne and vase,
Blue pottery, alabaster, and gold.   10

But dreamless long-dead Amen-hotep lies.
This is a dream of Winter, sweet as Spring.

Tall Nettles

Tall nettles cover up, as they have done
These many springs, the rusty harrow, the plough
Long worn out, and the roller made of stone:
Only the elm butt tops the nettles now.

This corner of the farmyard I like most:
As well as any bloom upon a flower
I like the dust on the nettles, never lost
Except to prove the sweetness of a shower.

Aspens

All day and night, save winter, every weather,
Above the inn, the smithy, and the shop,
The aspens at the cross-roads talk together
Of rain, until their last leaves fall from the top.

Out of the blacksmith's cavern comes the ringing
Of hammer, shoe, and anvil; out of the inn
The clink, the hum, the roar, the random singing—
The sounds that for these fifty years have been.

The whisper of the aspens is not drowned,
And over lightless pane and footless road,   10
Empty as sky, with every other sound
Not ceasing, calls their ghosts from their abode,

A silent smithy, a silent inn, nor fails
In the bare moonlight or the thick-furred gloom,
In tempest or the night of nightingales,
To turn the cross-roads to a ghostly room.

And it would be the same were no house near.
Over all sorts of weather, men, and times,
Aspens must shake their leaves and men may hear
But need not listen, more than to my rhymes.   20

Whatever wind blows, while they and I have leaves
We cannot other than an aspen be
That ceaselessly, unreasonably grieves,
Or so men think who like a different tree.

The Glory

The glory of the beauty of the morning,—
The cuckoo crying over the untouched dew;
The blackbird that has found it, and the dove
That tempts me on to something sweeter than love;
White clouds ranged even and fair as new-mown hay;
The heat, the stir, the sublime vacancy
Of sky and meadow and forest and my own heart:—
The glory invites me, yet it leaves me scorning
All I can ever do, all I can be,
Beside the lovely of motion, shape, and hue,   10
The happiness I fancy fit to dwell
In beauty's presence. Shall I now this day
Begin to seek as far as heaven, as hell,
Wisdom or strength to match this beauty, start
And tread the pale dust pitted with small dark drops,
In hope to find whatever it is I seek,
Hearkening to short-lived happy-seeming things
That we know naught of, in the hazel copse?
Or must I be content with discontent
As larks and swallows are perhaps with wings?   20
And shall I ask at the day's end once more
What beauty is, and what I can have meant
By happiness? And shall I let all go,
Glad, weary, or both? Or shall I perhaps know
That I was happy oft and oft before,
Awhile forgetting how I am fast pent,
How dreary-swift, with naught to travel to,
Is Time? I cannot bite the day to the core.

October

The green elm with the one great bough of gold
Lets leaves into the grass slip, one by one,—
The short hill grass, the mushrooms small, milk-
   white,
Harebell and scabious and tormentil,
That blackberry and gorse, in dew and sun,
Bow down to; and the wind travels too light
To shake the fallen birch leaves from the fern;
The gossamers wander at their own will.
At heavier steps than birds' the squirrels scold.
The late year has grown fresh again and new   10
As Spring and to the touch is not more cool
Than it is warm to the gaze; and now I might
As happy be as earth is beautiful,
Were I some other or with earth could turn
In alternation of violet and rose,
Harebell and snowdrop, at their season due,
And gorse that has no time not to be gay.
But if this be not happiness,—who knows?
Some day I shall think this a happy day,
And this mood by the name of melancholy   20
Shall no more blackened and obscured be.

Home

Often I had gone this way before:
But now it seemed I never could be
And never had been anywhere else:

'Twas home; one nationality
We had, I and the birds that sang,
One memory.

They welcomed me. I had come back
That eve somehow from somewhere far:
The April mist, the chill, the calm,
Meant the same thing familiar   10
And pleasant to us, and strange too,
Yet with no bar.

The thrush on the oaktop in the lane
Sang his last song, or last but one;
And as he ended, on the elm
Another had but just begun
His last; they knew no more than I
The day was done.

Then past his dark white cottage front
A labourer went along, his tread   20
Slow, half with weariness, half with ease;
And, through the silence, from his shed
The sound of sawing rounded all
That silence said.

Roads

I love roads:
The goddesses that dwell
Far along them invisible
Are my favourite gods.

Roads go on
While we forget, and are
Forgotten like a star
That shoots and is gone.

On this earth 'tis sure
We men have not made   10
Anything that doth fade
So soon, so long endure:

The hill road wet with rain
In the sun would not gleam
Like a winding stream
If we trod it not again.

They are lonely
While we sleep, lonelier
For lack of the traveller
Who is now a dream only.   20

From dawn's twilight
And all the clouds like sheep
On the mountains of sleep
They wind into the night.

The next turn may reveal
Heaven: upon the crest
The close pine clump, at rest
And black, may Hell conceal.

Often footsore, never
Yet of the road I weary,   30

Though long and steep and dreary,
As it winds on for ever.

Helen of the roads,
The mountain ways of Wales
And the Mabinogion tales
Is one of the true gods,

Abiding in the trees,
The threes and fours so wise,
The larger companies,
That by the roadside be,   40

And beneath the rafter
Else uninhabited
Excepting by the dead;
And it is her laughter

At morn and night I hear
When the thrush cock sings
Bright irrelevant things,
And when the chanticleer

Calls back to their own night
Troops that make loneliness   50
With their light footsteps' press,
As Helen's own are light.

Now all roads lead to France
And heavy is the tread
Of the living; but the dead
Returning lightly dance:

Whatever the road bring
To me or take from me,
They keep me company
With their pattering,   60

Crowding the solitude
Of the loops over the downs,
Hushing the roar of towns
And their brief multitude.

Old Man

Old Man, or Lad's-love—in the name there's nothing
To one that knows not Lad's-love, or Old Man,
The hoar-green feathery herb, almost a tree,
Growing with rosemary and lavender.
Even to one that knows it well, the names
Half decorate, half perplex, the thing it is:
At least, what that is clings not to the names
In spite of time. And yet I like the names.

The herb itself I like not, but for certain
I love it, as some day the child will love it   10
Who plucks a feather from the door-side bush
Whenever she goes in or out of the house.
Often she waits there, snipping the tips and
       shrivelling
The shreds at last on to the path, perhaps
Thinking, perhaps of nothing, till she sniffs
Her fingers and runs off. The bush is still
But half as tall as she, though it is as old;

So well she clips it. Not a word she says;
And I can only wonder how much hereafter
She will remember, with that bitter scent,   20
Of garden rows, and ancient damson trees
Topping a hedge, a bent path to a door,
A low thick bush beside the door, and me
Forbidding her to pick.

                                As for myself,
Where first I met the bitter scent is lost.
I, too, often shrivel the grey shreds,
Sniff them and think and sniff again and try
Once more to think what it is I am remembering,
Always in vain. I cannot like the scent,
Yet I would rather give up others more sweet,   30
With no meaning, than this bitter one.

I have mislaid the key. I sniff the spray
And think of nothing; I see and I hear nothing;
Yet seem, too, to be listening, lying in wait
For what I should, yet never can, remember:
No garden appears, no path, no hoar-green bush
Of Lad's-love, or Old Man, no child beside,
Neither father nor mother, nor any playmate;
Only an avenue, dark, nameless, without end.

Words

          Out of us all
          That make rhymes,
          Will you choose
          Sometimes—

As the winds use
A crack in a wall
Or a drain,
Their joy or their pain
To whistle through—
Choose me,   10
You English words?

I know you:
You are light as dreams,
Tough as oak,
Precious as gold,
As poppies and corn,
Or an old cloak;
Sweet as our birds
To the ear,
As the burnet rose   20
In the heat
Of Midsummer:
Strange as the races
Of dead and unborn:
Strange and sweet
Equally,
And familiar,
To the eye,
As the dearest faces
That a man knows,   30
And as lost homes are:
But though older far
Than oldest yew,—
As our hills are, old,—
Worn new

Again and again:
Young as our streams
After rain:
And as dear
As the earth which you prove   40
That we love.

Make me content
With some sweetness
From Wales
Whose nightingales
Have no wings,—
From Wiltshire and Kent
And Herefordshire,
And the villages there,—
From the names, and the things   50
No less.
Let me sometimes dance
With you,
Or climb
Or stand perchance
In ecstasy,
Fixed and free
In a rhyme,
As poets do.

Lights Out

I have come to the borders of sleep,
The unfathomable deep
Forest where all must lose
Their way, however straight,

Or winding, soon or late;
They cannot choose.

Many a road and track
That, since the dawn's first crack,
Up to the forest brink,
Deceived the travellers,   10
Suddenly now blurs,
And in they sink.

Here love ends,
Despair, ambition ends:
All pleasure and all trouble,
Although most sweet or bitter,
Here ends in sleep that is sweeter
Than tasks most noble.

There is not any book
Or face of dearest look   20
That I would not turn from now
To go into the unknown
I must enter, and leave, alone,
I know not how.

The tall forest towers;
Its cloudy foliage lowers
Ahead, shelf above shelf;
Its silence I hear and obey
That I may lose my way
And myself.   30

The Other

The forest ended. Glad I was
To feel the light, and hear the hum
Of bees, and smell the drying grass
And the sweet mint, because I had come
To an end of forest, and because
Here was both road and inn, the sum
Of what's not forest. But 'twas here
They asked me if I did not pass
Yesterday this way. "Not you? Queer."
"Who then? and slept here?" I felt fear.   10

I learnt his road and, ere they were
Sure I was I, left the dark wood
Behind, kestrel and woodpecker,
The inn in the sun, the happy mood
When first I tasted sunlight there.
I travelled fast, in hopes I should
Outrun that other. What to do
When caught, I planned not. I pursued
To prove the likeness, and, if true,
To watch until myself I knew.   20

I tried the inns that evening
Of a long gabled high-street grey,
Of courts and outskirts, travelling
An eager but a weary way,
In vain. He was not there. Nothing
Told me that ever till that day
Had one like me entered those doors,

Save once. That time I dared: "You may
Recall"—but never-foamless shores
Make better friends than those dull boors.　30

Many and many a day like this
Aimed at the unseen moving goal
And nothing found but remedies
For all desire. These made not whole;
They sowed a new desire, to kiss
Desire's self beyond control,
Desire of desire. And yet
Life stayed on within my soul.
One night in sheltering from the wet
I quite forgot I could forget.　40

A customer, then the landlady
Stared at me. With a kind of smile
They hesitated awkwardly:
Their silence gave me time for guile.
Had anyone called there like me,
I asked. It was quite plain the wile
Succeeded. For they poured out all.
And that was naught. Less than a mile
Beyond the inn, I could recall
He was like me in general.　50

He had pleased them, but I less.
I was more eager than before
To find him out and to confess,
To bore him and to let him bore.
I could not wait: children might guess
I had a purpose, something more
That made an answer indiscreet.

One girl's caution made me sore,
Too indignant even to greet
That other had we chanced to meet.   60

I sought then in solitude.
The wind had fallen with the night; as still
The roads lay as the ploughland rude,
Dark and naked, on the hill.
Had there been ever any feud
'Twixt earth and sky, a mighty will
Closed it: the crocketed dark trees,
A dark house, dark impossible
Cloud-towers, one star, one lamp, one peace
Held on an everlasting lease: 70

And all was earth's, or all was sky's;
No difference endured between
The two. A dog barked on a hidden rise;
A marshbird whistled high unseen;
The latest waking blackbird's cries
Perished upon the silence keen.
The last light filled a narrow firth
Among the clouds. I stood serene,
And with a solemn quiet mirth,
An old inhabitant of earth.   80

Once the name I gave to hours
Like this was melancholy, when
It was not happiness and powers
Coming like exiles home again,
And weaknesses quitting their bowers,
Smiled and enjoyed, far off from men,
Moments of everlastingness.

And fortunate my search was then
While what I sought, nevertheless,
That I was seeking, I did not guess.   90

That time was brief: once more at inn
And upon road I sought my man
Till once amid a tap-room's din
Loudly he asked for me, began
To speak, as if it had been a sin,
Of how I thought and dreamed and ran
After him thus, day after day:
He lived as one under a ban
For this: what had I got to say?
I said nothing. I slipped away.   100

And now I dare not follow after
Too close. I try to keep in sight,
Dreading his frown and worse his laughter.
I steal out of the wood to light;
I see the swift shoot from the rafter
By the inn door: ere I alight
I wait and hear the starlings wheeze
And nibble like ducks: I wait his flight.
He goes: I follow: no release
Until he ceases. Then I also shall cease.   110

Out in the dark

Out in the dark over the snow
The fallow fawns invisible go
With the fallow doe;

And the winds blow
Fast as the stars are slow.

Stealthily the dark haunts round
And, when the lamp goes, without sound
At a swifter bound
Than the swiftest hound,
Arrives, and all else is drowned;   10

And star and I and wind and deer,
Are in the dark together,—near,
Yet far,—and fear
Drums on my ear
In that sage company drear.

How weak and little is the light,
All the universe of sight,
Love and delight,
Before the might,
If you love it not, of night.   20

W. B. YEATS (1865-1939)

The leading figure in the Irish literary renaissance.
Born at Sandymount, near Dublin. Educated
Godolphin School, Hammersmith, and Erasmus
Smith School, Dublin. Art student for three years, but
left art for literature. Helped to found the Abbey
Theatre, Irish National Theatre (1899). Senator of the
Irish Free State, 1922–28. Awarded the Nobel Prize for
Literature, 1923. Works include: *The Wanderings of
Oisin* (1889); *The Countess Cathleen* (1892); *The Celtic
Twilight* (1893)—essays; *Poems* (1895); *Collected Prose*
(1908); *Plays for an Irish Theatre* (1912); *Later Poems*
(1923); *The Tower* (1928); *The Winding Stair* (1929);
Collected Poems (1933); *Collected Plays* (1934); *A Full
Moon in March* (1935); Editor *The Oxford Book of
Modern Verse* (1937); *New Poems* (1938); *Last Poems*
(1939); *Last Poems and Plays* (1940).

Beginning as a writer of poems of fantasy and Celtic
legend, W. B. Yeats became a poet writing of contemporary events as a result of the Easter Week
Risings in Dublin in 1916 and their subsequent
developments. Although he wrote of myth with concreteness and precision of epithet, it was the Irish
movement for independence that made Yeats into a
poet facing the reality of contemporary life. Not at
first identifying himself with this movement, he soon
came to do so when he found his friends involved.
Although the rebellion of Easter 1916 was a failure, it
can be said to be the beginning of modern Ireland. The
self-sacrifice of its leaders made a deep impression on
the Irish people, including Yeats, though he dis-

approved of the shedding of blood. To Yeats the
affair seemed to have changed his life and he wrote of
it feelingly and with a shocked sympathy. Always in
his mind and his poetry till then had been predominant
the conflict between things as they are—reality—and
things as they might be—the ideal.

> What the world's million lips are searching for
> Must be substantial somewhere.

But now this romantic ideal was put behind him and
he faced reality. It was his aim

> To write for my own race
> And for the reality.

Now he recognized the actual world, though he still
recalled the world of aristocratic elegance and order
that he had known at Coole.

In his latest verse Yeats upheld the standards of this
aristocratic refinement against much of the mean and
the common that he found distasteful in modern life,
where "all things at one common level lie"—its vulgarity, its cheap, newspaper-fed sentiments, its middle-
class caution, its demagogues, its commercial and
materialistic outlook, its worship of science, its physical violence, its chaos. He condemned those who
refused to live to the full because "everything that
lives is holy." His poetry is noble because it believes in
the importance of the primary virtues: courage,
loyalty, courtesy, humility, anger against stupidity or
injustice, belief in liberty and the rights of the
individual.

With this interest in public affairs, Yeats's style
matured as his ironic indignation grew. His language
assumed the rhythms of common speech. It became
bare and elliptical, simple and direct, every word

charged with meaning. His imagery was plain and vivid, his diction terse and concentrated. His rhythms were simple and strong, and his whole style epigrammatic and austere.

An Irish Airman foresees his Death

I know that I shall meet my fate
Somewhere among the clouds above;
Those that I fight I do not hate,
Those that I guard I do not love;
My country is Kiltartan Cross,
My countrymen Kiltartan's poor,
No likely end could bring them loss
Or leave them happier than before.
Nor law, nor duty bade me fight,
Nor public men, nor cheering crowds,   10

A lonely impulse of delight
Drove to this tumult in the clouds;
I balanced all, brought all to mind,
The years to come seemed waste of breath,
A waste of breath the years behind
In balance with this life, this death.

Easter 1916

I have met them at close of day
Coming with vivid faces
From counter or desk among grey
Eighteenth-century houses.
I have passed with a nod of the head
Or polite meaningless words,
Or have lingered awhile and said
Polite meaningless words,
And thought before I had done

Of a mocking tale or a gibe   10
To please a companion
Around the fire at the club,
Being certain that they and I
But lived where motley is worn:
All changed, changed utterly:
A terrible beauty is born.

That woman's days were spent
In ignorant good-will,
Her nights in argument
Until her voice grew shrill.   20
What voice more sweet than hers
When, young and beautiful,
She rode to harriers?
This man had kept a school
And rode our wingèd horse;
This other his helper and friend
Was coming into his force;
He might have won fame in the end,
So sensitive his nature seemed,
So daring and sweet his thought.   30
This other man I had dreamed
A drunken, vainglorious lout.
He had done most bitter wrong
To some who are near my heart,
Yet I number him in the song;
He, too, has resigned his part
In the casual comedy;
He, too, has been changed in his turn,
Transformed utterly:
A terrible beauty is born.   40

Hearts with one purpose alone
Through summer and winter seem
Enchanted to a stone
To trouble the living stream.
The horse that comes from the road,
The rider, the birds that range
From cloud to tumbling cloud,
Minute by minute they change;
A shadow of cloud on the stream
Changes minute by minute;   50
A horse-hoof slides on the brim,
And a horse plashes within it;
The long-legged moor-hens dive,
And hens to moor-cocks call;
Minute by minute they live:
The stone's in the midst of all.

Too long a sacrifice
Can make a stone of the heart.
O when may it suffice?
That is Heaven's part, our part   60
To murmur name upon name,
As a mother names her child
When sleep at last has come
On limbs that had run wild.
What is it but nightfall?
No, no, not night but death;
Was it needless death after all?
For England may keep faith
For all that is done and said.
We know their dream; enough   70
To know they dreamed and are dead;

And what if excess of love
Bewildered them till they died?
I write it out in a verse—
MacDonagh and MacBride
And Connolly and Pearse
Now and in time to be,
Wherever green is worn,
Are changed, changed utterly:
A terrible beauty is born.   80

The Second Coming

Turning and turning in the widening gyre
The falcon cannot hear the falconer;
Things fall apart; the centre cannot hold;
Mere anarchy is loosed upon the world,
The blood-dimmed tide is loosed, and everywhere
The ceremony of innocence is drowned;
The best lack all conviction, while the worst
Are full of passionate intensity.

Surely some revelation is at hand;
Surely the Second Coming is at hand.   10
The Second Coming! Hardly are those words out
When a vast image out of *Spiritus Mundi*
Troubles my sight: somewhere in sands of the
     desert
A shape with lion body and the head of a man,
A gaze blank and pitiless as the sun,
Is moving its slow thighs, while all about it
Reel shadows of the indignant desert birds.

The darkness drops again; but now I know
That twenty centuries of stony sleep
Were vexed to nightmare by a rocking cradle,   20
And what rough beast, its hour come round at last,
Slouches towards Bethlehem to be born?

Coole Park and Ballylee, 1931

Under my window-ledge the waters race,
Otters below and moor-hens on the top,
Run for a mile undimmed in Heaven's face
Then darkening through 'dark' Raftery's 'cellar'
        drop,
Run underground, rise in a rocky place
In Coole demesne, and there to finish up
Spread to a lake and drop into a hole.
What's water but the generated soul?

Upon the border of that lake's a wood
Now all dry sticks under a wintry sun,   10
And in a copse of beeches there I stood,
For Nature's pulled her tragic buskin on
And all the rant's a mirror of my mood:
At sudden thunder of the mounting swan
I turned about and looked where branches break
The glittering reaches of the flooded lake.

Another emblem there! That stormy white
But seems a concentration of the sky;
And, like the soul, it sails into the sight
And in the morning's gone, no man knows why;   20

And is so lovely that it sets to right
What knowledge or its lack had set awry,
So arrogantly pure, a child might think
It can be murdered with a spot of ink.

Sound of a stick upon the floor, a sound
From somebody that toils from chair to chair;
Beloved books that famous hands have bound,
Old marble heads, old pictures everywhere;
Great rooms where travelled men and children found
Content or joy; a last inheritor   30
Where none has reigned that lacked a name and
    fame
Or out of folly into folly came.

A spot whereon the founders lived and died
Seemed once more dear than life; ancestral trees,
Or gardens rich in memory glorified
Marriages, alliances and families,
And every bride's ambition satisfied.
Where fashion or mere fantasy decrees
We shift about—all that great glory spent—
Like some poor Arab tribesman and his tent.   40

We were the last romantics—chose for theme
Traditional sanctity and loveliness;
Whatever's written in what poets name
The book of the people; whatever most can bless
The mind of man or elevate a rhyme;
But all is changed, that high horse riderless,
Though mounted in that saddle Homer rode
Where the swan drifts upon a darkening flood.

A Prayer for my Daughter

Once more the storm is howling, and half hid
Under this cradle-hood and coverlid
My child sleeps on. There is no obstacle
But Gregory's wood and one bare hill
Whereby the haystack- and roof-levelling wind,
Bred on the Atlantic, can be stayed;
And for an hour I have walked and prayed
Because of the great gloom that is in my mind.

I have walked and prayed for this young child an
        hour
And heard the sea-wind scream upon the tower,   10
And under the arches of the bridge, and scream
In the elms above the flooded stream;
Imagining in excited reverie
That the future years had come,
Dancing to a frenzied drum,
Out of the murderous innocence of the sea.

May she be granted beauty and yet not
Beauty to make a stranger's eye distraught,
Or hers before a looking-glass, for such,
Being made beautiful overmuch,   20
Consider beauty a sufficient end,
Lose natural kindness and maybe
The heart-revealing intimacy
That chooses right, and never find a friend.

Helen being chosen found life flat and dull
And later had much trouble from a fool,
While that great Queen, that rose out of the spray,
Being fatherless could have her way
Yet chose a bandy-leggèd smith for man.
It's certain that fine women eat   30
A crazy salad with their meat
Whereby the Horn of Plenty is undone.

In courtesy I'd have her chiefly learned;
Hearts are not had as a gift but hearts are earned
By those that are not entirely beautiful;
Yet many, that have played the fool
For beauty's very self, has charm made wise,
And many a poor man that has roved,
Loved and thought himself beloved,
From a glad kindness cannot take his eyes.   40

May she become a flourishing hidden tree
That all her thoughts may like the linnet be,
And have no business but dispensing round
Their magnanimities of sound,
Nor but in merriment begin a chase,
Nor but in merriment a quarrel.
O may she live like some green laurel
Rooted in one dear perpetual place.

My mind, because the minds that I have loved,
The sort of beauty that I have approved,   50
Prosper but little, has dried up of late,
Yet knows that to be choked with hate
May well be of all evil chances chief.

If there's no hatred in a mind
Assault and battery of the wind
Can never tear the linnet from the leaf.

An intellectual hatred is the worst,
So let her think opinions are accursed.
Have I not seen the loveliest woman born
Out of the mouth of Plenty's horn,   60
Because of her opinionated mind
Barter that horn and every good
By quiet natures understood
For an old bellows full of angry wind?

Considering that, all hatred driven hence,
The soul recovers radical innocence
And learns at last that it is self-delighting,
Self-appeasing, self-affrighting,
And that its own sweet will is Heaven's will;
She can, though every face should scowl   70
And every windy quarter howl
Or every bellows burst, be happy still.

And may her bridegroom bring her to a house
Where all's accustomed, ceremonious;
For arrogance and hatred are the wares
Peddled in the thoroughfares.
How but in custom and in ceremony
Are innocence and beauty born?
Ceremony's a name for the rich horn,
And custom for the spreading laurel tree.   80

Sailing to Byzantium

That is no country for old men. The young
In one another's arms, birds in the trees
—Those dying generations—at their song,
The salmon-falls, the mackerel-crowded seas,
Fish, flesh, or fowl, commend all summer long
Whatever is begotten, born, and dies.
Caught in that sensual music all neglect
Monuments of unageing intellect.

An aged man is but a paltry thing,
A tattered coat upon a stick, unless   10
Soul clap its hands and sing, and louder sing
For every tatter in its mortal dress,
Nor is there singing school but studying
Monuments of its own magnificence;
And therefore I have sailed the seas and come
To the holy city of Byzantium.

O sages standing in God's holy fire
As in the gold mosaic of a wall,
Come from the holy fire, perne in a gyre,
And be the singing-masters of my soul.   20
Consume my heart away; sick with desire
And fastened to a dying animal
It knows not what it is; and gather me
Into the artifice of eternity.

Once out of nature I shall never take
My bodily form from any natural thing,

But such a form as Grecian goldsmiths make
Of hammered gold and gold enamelling
To keep a drowsy Emperor awake;
Or set upon a golden bough to sing   30
To lords and ladies of Byzantium
Of what is past, or passing, or to come.

Byzantium

The unpurged images of day recede;
The Emperor's drunken soldiery are abed;
Night resonance recedes, night-walker's song
After great cathedral gong;
A starlit or a moonlit dome disdains
All that man is,
All mere complexities,
The fury and the mire of human veins.

Before me floats an image, man or shade,
Shade more than man, more image than a shade;   10
For Hades' bobbin bound in mummy-cloth
May unwind the winding path;
A mouth that has no moisture and no breath
Breathless mouths may summon;
I hail the superhuman;
I call it death-in-life and life-in-death.

Miracle, bird or golden handiwork,
More miracle than bird or handiwork,
Planted on the star-lit golden bough,
Can like the cocks of Hades crow,   20

Or, by the moon embittered, scorn aloud
In glory of changeless metal
Common bird or petal
And all complexities of mire or blood.

At midnight on the Emperor's pavement flit
Flames that no faggot feeds, nor steel has lit,
Nor storm disturbs, flames begotten of flame,
Where blood-begotten spirits come
And all complexities of fury leave,
Dying into a dance,   30
An agony of trance,
An agony of flame that cannot singe a sleeve.

Astraddle on the dolphin's mire and blood,
Spirit after spirit! The smithies break the flood,
The golden smithies of the Emperor!
Marbles of the dancing floor
Break bitter furies of complexity,
Those images that yet
Fresh images beget,
That dolphin-torn, that gong-tormented sea.   40

An Acre of Grass

Picture and book remain,
An acre of green grass
For air and exercise,
Now strength of body goes;
Midnight, an old house
Where nothing stirs but a mouse.

My temptation is quiet.
Here at life's end
Neither loose imagination,
Nor the mill of the mind   10
Consuming its rag and bone,
Can make the truth known.

Grant me an old man's frenzy,
Myself must I remake
Till I am Timon and Lear
Or that William Blake
Who beat upon the wall
Till Truth obeyed his call;

A mind Michael Angelo knew
That can pierce the clouds,   20
Or inspired by frenzy
Shake the dead in their shrouds;
Forgotten else by mankind,
An old man's eagle mind.

ANDREW YOUNG (1885–1971)

Born in Elgin. Educated at the Royal High School, Edinburgh, and at Edinburgh University. He was a Canon of Chichester Cathedral from 1948, and Vicar of Stonegate, Sussex, 1941–59. Works include: *Boaz and Ruth* (1920); *The Cuckoo Clock* (1922); *Winter Harvest* (1933); *Collected Poems* (1936); *Nicodemus: A Play in Verse* (1937); *Speak to the Earth* (1940); *The Green Man* (1947); *Collected Poems* (1948); *A Prospect of Flowers* (1945) and *A Prospect of Britain* (1956)—prose; *Into Hades* (1952); *Quiet as Moss* (1959).

In his poems as in his prose works Andrew Young is a lover of the English countryside: "I made myself as a tree."

> I was content . . .
> To stand in breathless hush
> With no more life myself than tree or bush.

With accurate observation, patient responsiveness and imaginative sympathy, he reveals an intimacy with the creatures and vegetation of the countryside that has the ring of authenticity and shows the familiar in a new light. These are no poems written from the seclusion of the study and based on second-hand information derived from books about Nature; they have the breath of the open-air, the note of one who stands beside a tree and watches fox cubs or March hares or lambs at play. Accurate and fresh in observation, the poet yet remains detached and objective, thus avoiding the romantic or the sentimental note. With a strong feeling for place is linked a perception of time, of the history that lies behind every meadow and wood and hill. The past of the countryside is part of the present, and "the living spirit within" shines through.

A mastery of exact detail is allied with the ability to pinpoint it in the terse and lucid phrase and in a simple and unobtrusive rhythm. The result has often the surprise of an epigram.

> Lane that eases the sharp-scarped hill
> Winding the slope with leisurely will.

> Pale lambs leap with their leggings on
> Over small hills that are not there.

> That slant-legged robin
> With autumn on his chest.

Although the subjects of the poems may at first sight appear slight, they are never trivial and they are given depth and significance because, with the eye of both a child and a sage, the poet sees the mysterious in the familiar, the eternal in the transient, and the past and the present as one.

> Foot of Briton, formal Roman,
> Saxon and Dane and Sussex yeoman
> Have delved it deep as river-bed.

A poet-cleric, Andrew Young had his roots as deeply-based in the countryside of England as his predecessors, Herrick, Herbert, and Vaughan, and as R. S. Thomas to-day. We listen while he meditates aloud.

March Hares

I made myself as a tree,
No withered leaf twirling on me;
No, not a bird that stirred my boughs,
As looking out from wizard brows
I watched those lithe and lovely forms
That raised the leaves in storms.

I watched them leap and run,
Their bodies hollowed in the sun
To thin transparency,
That I could clearly see
The shallow colour of their blood
Joyous in love's full flood.

I was content enough,
Watching that serious game of love,
That happy hunting in the wood
Where the pursuer was the more pursued,
To stand in breathless hush
With no more life myself than tree or bush.

The Stockdoves

They rose up in a twinkling cloud
And wheeled about and bowed
To settle on the trees
Perching like small clay images.

Then with a noise of sudden rain
They clattered off again
And over Ballard Down
They circled like a flying town.

Though one could sooner blast a rock
Than scatter that dense flock   10
That through the winter weather
Some iron rule has held together,

Yet in another month from now
Love like a spark will blow
Those birds the country over
To drop in trees, lover by lover.

The Dead Crab

A rosy shield upon its back,
That not the hardest storm could crack,
From whose sharp edge projected out
Black pin-point eyes staring about;
Beneath, the well-knit cote-armure
That gave to its weak belly power;
The clustered legs with plated joints
That ended in stiletto points;
The claws like mouths it held outside:—
I cannot think this creature died   10
By storm or fish or sea-fowl harmed
Walking the sea so heavily armed;
Or does it make for death to be
Oneself a living armoury?

Field-glasses

Though buds still speak in hints
And frozen ground has set the flints
As fast as precious stones
And birds perch on the boughs, silent as cones,

Suddenly waked from sloth
Young trees put on a ten years' growth
And stones double their size,
Drawn nearer through field-glasses' greater eyes.

Why I borrow their sight
Is not to give small birds a fright   10
Creeping up close by inches;
I make the trees come, bringing tits and finches.

I lift a field itself
As lightly as I might a shelf,
And the rooks do not rage
Caught for a moment in my crystal cage.

And while I stand and look,
Their private lives an open book,
I feel so privileged
My shoulders prick, as though they were half-
    fledged.   20

The Lane

Years and years and man's thoughtful foot,
Drip and guttering rains and mute
Shrinkage of snows, and shaggy-hoofed
Horse have sunk this lane tree-roofed
　　Now patched with blossoming elder,
　　　Wayfaring-tree and guelder;
Lane that eases the sharp-scarped hill
Winding the slope with leisurely will.

Foot of Briton, formal Roman,
Saxon and Dane and Sussex yeoman   10
Have delved it deep as river-bed,
Till I walk wading to my head
　　In air so close and hot
　　　And by the wind forgot,
It seems to me that in this place
The earth is breathing on my face.

Here I loiter a lost hour,
Listen to bird, look on a flower.
What will be left when I am gone?
A trodden root, a loosened stone   20
　　And by the blackthorn caught
　　　Some gossamery thought
Of thankfulness to those dead bones
That knit hills closer than loose stones.

Wood and Hill

Nowhere is one alone
And in the closest covert least,
But to small eye of bird or beast
He will be known;
To-day it was for me
A squirrel that embraced a tree
Turning a small head round;
A hare too that ran up the hill,
To his short forelegs level ground,
And with tall ears stood still.   10
But it was birds I could not see
And larks that tried to stand on air
That made of wood and hill a market-square.

The Secret Wood

Where there is nothing more to see
Than this old earth-bound tree
That years ago dry sawdust bled
But sprouts each spring a leaf or two
As though it tried not to be dead,
Or that down-hanging broken bough
That keeps its withered leaves till now,
Like a dead man that cannot move
Or take his own clothes off,
What is it that I seek or who,   10
Fearing from passer-by
Intrusion of a foot or eye?

I only know
Though all men of earth's beauty speak
Beauty here I do not seek
More than I sought it on my mother's cheek.

Late Autumn

The boy called to his team
    And with blue-glancing share
Turned up the rape and turnip
    With yellow charlock to spare.

The long lean thistles stood
    Like beggars ragged and blind,
Half their white silken locks
    Blown away on the wind.

But I thought not once of winter
    Or summer that was past   10
Till I saw that slant-legged robin
    With autumn on his chest.

Hard Frost

Frost called to water "Halt!"
And crusted the moist snow with sparkling salt;
Brooks, their own bridges, stop,
And icicles in long stalactites drop,
And tench in water-holes
Lurk under gluey glass like fish in bowls.

In the hard-rutted lane
At every footstep breaks a brittle pane,
And tinkling trees ice-bound,
Changed into weeping willows, sweep the ground; 10
Dead boughs take root in ponds
And ferns on windows shoot their ghostly fronds.

But vainly the fierce frost
Interns poor fish, ranks trees in an armed host,
Hangs daggers from house-eaves
And on the windows ferny ambush weaves;
In the long war grown warmer
The sun will strike him dead and strip his armour.

Last Snow

Although the snow still lingers
Heaped on the ivy's blunt webbed fingers
And painted tree-trunks on one side,
Here in this sunlit ride
The fresh unchristened things appear,
Leaf, spathe and stem,
With crumbs of earth clinging to them
To show the way they came
But no flower yet to tell their name,
And one green spear   10
Stabbing a dead leaf from below
Kills winter at a blow.

A Prehistoric Camp

It was the time of year
    Pale lambs leap with thick leggings on
Over small hills that are not there,
    That I climbed Eggardon.

The hedgerows still were bare,
    None ever knew so late a year;
Birds build their nests in the open air,
    Love conquering their fear.

But there on the hill-crest,
    Where only larks or stars look down,   10
Earthworks exposed a vaster nest,
    Its race of men long flown.

Wiltshire Downs

The cuckoo's double note
Loosened like bubbles from a drowning throat
Floats through the air
In mockery of pipit, lark and stare.

The stable-boys thud by
Their horses slinging divots at the sky
And with bright hooves
Printing the sodden turf with lucky grooves.

As still as a windhover
A shepherd in his flapping coat leans over   10
His tall sheep-crook
And shearlings, tegs and yoes cons like a book.

And one tree-crowned long barrow
Stretched like a sow that has brought forth her
     farrow
Hides a king's bones
Lying like broken sticks among the stones.

The Roman Wall

Though moss and lichen crawl
    These square-set stones still keep their serried
       ranks
Guarding the ancient wall,
    That whitlow-grass with lively silver pranks.

Time they could not keep back
    More than the wind that from the snow-streaked
       north
Taking the air for track
    Flows lightly over to the south shires forth.

Each stone might be a cist
    Where memory sleeps in dust and nothing tells   10
More than the silent mist
    That smokes along the heather-blackened fells.

Twitching its ears as pink
   As blushing scallops loved by Romans once
A lamb leaps to its drink
   And, as the quavering cry breaks on the stones,

Time like a leaf down-drops
   And pacing by the stars and thorn-trees' sough
A Roman sentry stops
   And hears the water lapping on Crag Lough.   20

NOTES

Musée des Beaux Arts (*p.* 17)

What seems to Auden admirable in Brueghel's painting of "Icarus" is that the painter should have shown everyday life going on steadily, unconscious that Icarus is falling to his death. It is this very contrast between the personal sorrow and the ever-flowing stream of life that, according to the poet, gives this event its peculiar pathos.

2. *The Old Masters:* classical painters.

14. *Brueghel's Icarus:* Icarus was son of Daedalus. He flew with his father from Crete; but the sun melted the wax with which his wings were fastened on and he fell into the sea and was drowned. Compare 3 *Henry VI*, v. 6. 18–25:

> GLOUCESTER: Why, what a peevish fool was that of Crete,
>   That taught his son the office of a fowl!
>   And yet, for all his wings, the fool was drowned.
> KING HENRY: I, Daedalus; my poor boy, Icarus;
>   Thy father, Minos, that denied our course;
>   The sun, that seared the wings of my sweet boy,
>   Thy brother Edward, and thyself the sea,
>   Whose envious gulf did swallow up his life.

This legend forms the subject of a painting by Pieter Brueghel (*c.* 1525–69), the Flemish painter. His roystering scenes of peasants eating and drinking, dancing and courting, his landscapes that praise earth and sky for their own sake and not as backgrounds for romantic ruined castles, his sunlit harvest scenes, and his grim records of winter, all have subtlety of design, great powers of observation, firm drawing, and an unusual facility in combining great sweeping compositions with minute depiction of detail.

The Novelist (*p.* 18)

This is an adaptation of the kind of sonnet that Rilke used to write. Rainer Maria Rilke (1875–1926) was an Austrian poet, now generally considered to have been one of the greatest lyric poets in German literature. He wrote also a strongly autobiographical novel. His letters are important as expressing his artistry and philosophy of life. Compare Auden's sonnets on *Edward Lear* and *The Composer*. Auden illuminates a complex life with economy and apt symbolism. He, like the novelist, has an absorbed interest in human motives and relationships. The most interesting subject for him is man, doubting, suffering, searching. He analyses the general type of novelist, rather than describes any particular one.

13–14. These lines can be applied to Auden himself.

O Love, the interest itself in thoughtless Heaven (*p.* 18)

5. *murmuration:* a murmuring, production of a low continuous sound.

8. *scarp:* the steep face of a hill.

9. *mole:* breakwater; *i.e.*, Britain.

10. *Newton:* Sir Isaac Newton (1642–1727), the philosopher and mathematician. His researches on light and colours were summed up in his *Optics* (1704), to which was appended his Method of Fluxions, his great mathematical discovery. His *Principia Mathematica*, embodying his laws of motion and the idea of universal gravitation (the idea of which was traditionally suggested to Newton by the sight of an apple falling from the tree), was published in 1687. He was elected President of the Royal Society in 1703 and annually re-elected. He was buried in Westminster Abbey.

20. *Dumbarton:* once a flourishing shipbuilding town.
21. *Rowley:* in Durham.
35. *Moel Fammau:* the highest point in the range of hills enclosing the Vale of Clwyd, North Denbighshire.
37. *ammonite:* a fossil with whorled, chambered shells; they were once thought to be coiled snakes petrified, and called snake-stone.
41. *Merlin:* the enchanter and soothsayer of Arthurian legend. He appears in Malory's *Morte d'Arthur* and Tennyson's *Idylls of the King.*
42. *Stonehenge:* the great prehistoric monument on Salisbury Plain. It was probably used (if not built) by the Druids, and it is thought to have been the temple of a sun-god and to have been built about 1680 B.C.
    the Pillars: the Pillars of Hercules; a name given to the two mountains opposite one another at the entrance of the Mediterranean, supposed to have been parted by the arm of Hercules; the Straits of Gibraltar.

Lay your sleeping head, my love (*p.* 21)

The poet tells of a night of love, but the beauty of that night is impaired by his consciousness that it has been snatched from chaos. The experience is related to its social setting.

Look, stranger, on this island now (*p.* 22)

One of Auden's few poems of natural description, his scenery being usually a background for some human situation, or a symbol; rarely has it much interest for the poet in itself. In the tide's movement, the gull's flight, and the ships' "saunter," the poet is attempting to combine sound and movement, sense and mood.

1st September 1939 (*p. 23*)

The conversational tone of the poem speaks directly to the reader in a grave but friendly manner.

On September 1, 1939, Germany invaded Poland, and two days later England and France declared war on Germany.

1. *dives:* illegal drinking-dens or places of low resort, often situated in a cellar (United States).

2. *Fifty-second Street:* a street in New York mainly with warehouses at one end and tenements at the other.

14. *Luther:* Martin Luther (1483–1546), leader of the Reformation in Germany.

15. *a culture:* of Germany.

16. *Linz:* capital of the Austrian Duchy. Hitler, whose father was a customs official there, was born in 1889 at a near-by village, Braunau-am-Inn.

17. *imago:* an interior type, a type founded upon real persons (in especial upon the father or the mother) and which, from the depths of our subconscious, continues to guide our actions and to stimulate our sympathies and our antipathies.

18. *psychopathic:* connected with mental disease or disorder.
    god: i.e., Hitler.

23. *Thucydides:* great Athenian historian (*c.* 460–*c.* 400 B.C.) His history, which deals with the Peloponnesian War, the great war between Athens and Sparta, down to the year 411, is concise and is marked by scrupulous accuracy. It is the first work of the kind in which events are traced to their cause and their political lessons brought out. He was exiled from 423 to 404 owing to failure as a naval commander.

29. *his book:* the history of the Peloponnesian War. See note above.

41. *euphoric:* of well-being.

59. *Nijinsky:* 1890–1950. He took command of the Russian Ballet in 1913. As a dancer, he was among the greatest in history, and his premature retirement in 1919, due to illness and later madness, was an irreparable loss to the ballet.

60. *Diaghilev:* the Russian ballet producer (1872–1929), who organized ballet and opera seasons in London, Paris, America, etc. Many of his productions were of amazing beauty.

69. *commuters:* season ticket holders.

96. *Eros:* Love (the god of Love, *i.e.,* Cupid).

Streams (*p.* 27)

5–6. The reference is to the four elements.

10. *vocables:* words, names.

12. *Babel:* the lofty structure in Genesis XI. 1–9, "a tower whose top may reach unto heaven."

23. *Iseult's tower:* in Arthurian romance, Iseult was the daughter of the King of Ireland, and the wife of Mark, King of Cornwall, but she loved Sir Tristram. Mark had sent his nephew, Tristram, on a ship to Ireland to bring his bride to Cornwall. *En route* they unwittingly drank the magic love-potion intended for Mark and Iseult. Their consequent tragic love for each other led to Tristram's finally going to Brittany.

24. *willow:* a symbol of unhappy or unrequited love. Compare *The Merchant of Venice*, V. I. 10–12:

> Stood Dido with a willow in her hand
> Upon the wild sea-bank and waft her love
> To come again to Carthage.

pash-notes: colloquially, notes of passion or violent affection.

25. *Homo Ludens:* playing, or sporting, man; a modification of the common phrase *Homo Sapiens* (thinking man), used to describe man as distinguished from the animals.

27-8. *Huppim to Muppim:* imaginary names for the two banks of the river.

28. *crankle:* turn, twist or wind.

30. *Brahma's son:* Brahma is one of the major gods of the Hindus, the creator. The river the Brahmaputra (in Sanskrit *putra* means 'son of') is a great river of South Asia flowing through Assam and helping to form a vast delta at the head of the Bay of Bengal.

31. *titanic:* gigantic, huge, vast. The Titans were a race of giants in mythology, children of Heaven and Earth, who carried on a long and fierce struggle with the Olympian gods.

32. *Assam:* a state in the north-east part of India.

   Himalayan: the Himalayas are the mountain chain forming the northern boundary of India and including Mount Everest.

41. *polis:* a city (Greek), a political unit, a commonwealth or state.

43. *Gaston Paris:* French scholar and Romance philologist, 1839-1903. He founded the *Revue Critique* in 1866, which helped to lead to a revival of scientific studies in France.

44. *Bismarck's siege-guns:* Bismarck, 1815-98, Prussian statesman, famous as the creator and the first chancellor of the German Empire. His foreign policy led to the Franco-Prussian War of 1870-71, during which Paris was besieged.

45. *that dale:* Swaledale in North Yorkshire, an upland dale with magnificent scenery and fishing, wild beauty, bold slopes and an impetuous stream.

46. *fell-side:* the rough hill-side.

   Kisdon Beck: a beck is a brook or stream, especially a brook with a stony bed or rugged course.

54. *monomaniac:* obsessed with one subject.

55. *megalith:* a huge stone or monument, usually found in a stone circle like Stonehenge.

    fossil: the petrified remains of an animal or vegetable found embedded in the strata of the earth's crust.

61. *armigers:* armour-bearers, esquires who attended knights to bear their armour.

Upper Lambourne (*p.* 33)

Upper Lambourne is a market town in Berkshire. It lies high up in the narrow valley of the Lambourne, a tributary of the Kennet, famous for its trout-fishing. Its chief importance is derived from the large racehorse training-stables in the neighbourhood.

9. *Cararra:* a town of Tuscany, Italy, famous for its marble quarries.

11. *He who trained a hundred winners:* The poet writes that he had no particular trainer in mind, but white marble monuments to various trainers are to be found in Upper Lambourne churchyard.

20. *sarsen:* the numerous large boulders or blocks of sandstone found scattered on the surface of the chalk downs, especially in Berkshire and Wiltshire.

Greenaway (*p.* 34)

11. *bladderwrack:* the seaweed which has air-bladders in it, fronds.

12. *Greenaway:* "a beach of shingle among rocks half-way between Trebetherick," writes Mr Betjeman, "where I spent my childhood in Cornwall, and Polzeath, the next village. Greenaway always has large waves at high tide and it looks out to the Atlantic."

20. *cowries:* small shells (used as money in many parts of Southern Asia and Africa).

East Anglian Bathe (*p. 35*)

2. *Horsey Mere:* on the Broads in Norfolk. It feeds the river Thurne, a tributary of the Bure. It is one-and-a-half miles from the sea. The Romans made Horsey a settlement. It still has a Norman church.

3. *bent-grass:* grass of a reedy kind; also, various grass-like reeds, rushes, and sedges.

Norfolk (*p. 36*)

7. *sorrel:* a small perennial plant, characterized by a sour taste, and to some extent cultivated for culinary purposes.

11. *alder:* a tree related to the birch and common in wet places.

16. *Bure:* a tributary of the Yare, joining it in the very streets of Yarmouth.

20. *the church:* of Coltishall.

21. *Fowler of Louth:* Joseph Fowler, 1791–1882, a church-restorer, born at Winterton, Lincolnshire. Among others he restored Louth Church, re-roofing the choir. He was a competent Gothic revivalist. "He did not 'restore' Coltishall Church," writes Mr Betjeman, "of which I was thinking when I wrote the poem, but he was a sort of Gothic revival architect who *would* have restored an East Anglian church. In fact, you may take him as symbolic."

Essex (*p. 37*)

4. *Benfleet:* a residential urban district five miles west of Southend. It has a Norman church and ruins of a thirteenth-century castle.

Leigh-on-Sea: part of Southend, a residential county borough on the North bank of the Thames estuary. Its tower has been a landmark to seamen for 400 years.

13. *Matching Tye:* to the North of Havering. One of the gems of the county with two greens, a medieval cottage, and a thirteenth-century church.

14. *Havering-atte-Bower:* West of Romford. Royal homes used to be in Havering Park. It has a big village green with stocks and a whipping-post of *c.* 1700.

   Stocks: a frame of timber with holes in which the ankles of petty offenders were confined. Still found in some villages.

21. *River Lea:* it rises in South Bedfordshire and joins the Thames at Blackwell. It flows past the boundary of Essex and Hertfordshire.

23. *Epping Forest:* a royal forest in South-west Essex, formerly called Waltham Forest. Open to the public as a pleasure-ground.

24. *beanfeasts:* annual dinners given by employers to their hands; here, jolly outings.

25. *convoluted:* with tortuous windings.

26. *brakes:* large wagonettes, open carriages built to carry about twelve persons on two back seats arranged length-wise and facing inwards.

35. *Great Eastern:* the old name for the section of railway running through Essex, later absorbed into the London and North Eastern Line, before the nationalization of British Railways.

37. *yarrow:* the plant milfoil, remarkable for the numerous divisions of its leaf. It is a perennial herb, with white flowers and a pungent odour.

Before the Anæsthetic (*p.* 40)

In this, the most personal poem John Betjeman has written, he comes as near as he has ever come to revealing his most intimate feelings.

2. *St Giles's:* the church near St John's College, Oxford.

17. *help from ages past:* an echo of the hymn, "O God our help in ages past," by Isaac Watts (1674–1748).

39. *missals:* books containing the service of the Mass, or Holy Communion. The word is used in the Church of England, especially among Anglo-Catholics.

40. *screens:* partitions of wood or stone, pierced by one or more doors, dividing a church into two parts, *e.g.*, chancel-screen, rood-screen.

  quires: choirs; the choir is a part of a church appropriated to the singers, the chancel.

The Listeners (*p.* 46)

The poem at first appears to be a rendering of that uncanny experience of approach to an empty and deserted house. But the atmosphere is more strange and ghostly, with more of mystery and terror, than such an experience would involve. With subtly diversified vowel sounds, the poem combines beauty of music and of word.

The Ghost (*p.* 47)

Stark despair is in this poem, the desolation of complete loss (l. 19). But some see in it, also, a consoling beauty: the tragedy of mortal love is both beautiful and desolating.

3. When the grave is described so, it suggests dew and fragrance rather than death and decay.

14. *the stars:* they suggest the loneliness and insignificance and helplessness of man; and at the same time they recall the dew and fragrance of l. 3.

Fare Well (*p.* 51)

This is a lyric of profound significance.

14. *Traveller's Joy:* so called because of its trailing over and adorning hedges by the wayside. The wild clematis; also called old man's beard. Note the connexion of the name of the flower with the thought of the poem.

All That's Past (*p. 52*)

The poem is a piece of enchantment, the subtle rhythm casting a spell. Mystery and wonder are created by the poem.

1–8. Echoes of the legend of the Sleeping Beauty.

8 *Roves back the rose:* the half-completed echo matches the romantic thought: it recalls the garlands woven by the Cavalier poets (*e.g.*, Waller's *Go, lovely rose*), by Spenser and Ronsard, the flowers that graced the Wars of the Roses, Venus in Greek and Latin verse, and the Rose of Bethlehem.

16. *Solomon:* the wise man and king of Israel (died about 930 B.C.).

24. *amaranth:* an imaginary flower that never fades. Among the ancients it was the symbol of immortality, because its flowers retained to the last much of their deep blood-red colour.

The Snowdrop (*p. 55*)

The poet asks the question, "What is God?" and to find the answer he tries to project his mind into the life of the snowdrop. He is partially successful, and finds God by a mystical process, and understands Him to the extent of discovering that both man and flower share in His nature. Compare Tennyson's:

> Little flower in the crannied wall,
> I pluck you out of the crannies;
> Hold you here, root and all, in my hand,
> Little flower—but if I could understand
> What you are, root and all, and all in all,
> I should know what God and man is.

Compare also Francis Thompson's *All Flesh*:

> Epitomized in thee [a grass-blade]
> Was the mystery
> Which shakes the spheres conjoint—
> God focussed to a point.

Polonius (*p.* 56)

This is one of ten poems, perceptive and subtle, on characters from Shakespeare; the others are Macbeth, Banquo, Falstaff, Hamlet, Ophelia, Iago, Mercutio, Imogen, and Juliet's Nurse. For Polonius, the foolish-wise counsellor of Claudius, King of Denmark, see *Hamlet*.

7. *a keyhole:* he met his death through eavesdropping. See IV. 3.

8. *His tenderness:* to his son, Laertes, and his daughter, Ophelia.

12–15. He sometimes utters good, sound, worldly wisdom, as in his speech to Laertes, I. 3. 58–80, especially the last three lines:

> These few precepts in thy memory
> Look thou character. Give thy thoughts no tongue . . .
> This above all: to thine own self be true,
> And it must follow, as the night the day,
> Thou canst not then be false to any man.

19. *Bacon:* Francis Bacon (1561–1626). Lord Chancellor 1618–21. A statesman and philosopher whose ideas had a great influence on seventeenth-century thought and led to the formation of the Royal Society. His chief works are *The New Atlantis* (1627), *The Advancement of Learning* (1605), and *Essays* (1597). Pope called him "the wisest, brightest, meanest of mankind."

A Portrait (*p.* 57)

A new note in observation faithfully recorded is struck in this recognizable self-portrait.

14. *dryad:* a nymph of the forests and trees.

15. *Crusoe:* a solitary man; the only inhabitant of a place. From the tale by Daniel Defoe (1661–1731), which describes Robinson Crusoe as cast on a desert island.

42. *the seven seas:* the Arctic and Antarctic, North and South Pacific, North and South Atlantic, and Indian Oceans.

43. *tales by idiot told:* compare *Macbeth* v. 5. 26–7:

> Life . . . is a tale
> Told by an idiot, full of sound and fury.

56. *Orpheus:* a Thracian poet of Greek legend, who could move even inanimate things by his music. When his wife Eurydice died he went into the infernal regions, and so charmed Pluto that she was released on the condition that Orpheus would not look back until they reached the earth. He was just about to place his foot on the earth when he turned round, and Eurydice vanished from him in an instant.

61. *A foolish fond old man:* compare *King Lear* iv. 7. 60: "I am a very foolish fond old man."

Journey of the Magi (*p.* 64)

The Magi were the three Wise Men who followed the Star of Bethlehem from the East to lay gifts before the infant Jesus. See Matthew ii.

The speaker is an old man. The event of which he was a witness marks the end of an old order and the beginning of a new, but the interim is full of doubt and pain. It has made the old order impossible and has upset the values by which one lived. The new is destructive of the old; the birth of

Christianity means the death of the old world. The old king has returned to his kingdom and finds his people clutching their gods, which were once his gods but are now alien to him. His discovery of the new faith is both reassuring and disconcerting. He waits impatiently for the release of bodily death.

The peculiar quality of the poem lies in its understatement ("it was, you may say, satisfactory"): the contrast between the conversational, matter-of-fact account and the importance and effect of the journey.

1–5. These lines are an adaptation from a sermon of Lancelot Andrewes (1555–1626), Bishop of Winchester. This sermon supplies the two basic ideas of the poem: Andrewes dwells first on the faith of the Wise Men and later asks what they found. "Before extracting all the spiritual meaning of a text, Andrewes forces a concrete presence upon us," says T. S. Eliot. Andrewes wrote:

> It was no summer progress. A cold coming they had of it at this time of the year, just the worst time of the year to take a journey, and specially a long journey in. The ways deep, the weather sharp, the days short, the sun farthest off, *in solstitio brumali*, 'the very dead of winter.'

10.   *sherbet:* a cooling fruit drink.

23.   Why, for all of us, out of all that we have heard, seen, felt, in a lifetime, do certain images recur, charged with emotion, rather than others? The song of one bird, the leap of one fish, at a particular place and time, . . . six ruffians seen through an open window playing cards at night at a small French railway-junction where there was a water-mill . . .

> T. S. Eliot: *The Use of Poetry and the Use of Criticism*

24. The three trees portend the trees to be lifted upon the hill outside the city walls of Jerusalem.

25. See the white horse in Revelation (VI. 2; XIX. 11).

27. A reference to the soldiers who diced for Christ's gar-

ments at the foot of the Cross (Matthew xxvii. 35); and to the thirty pieces of silver for which Judas betrayed Christ (Matthew xxvi. 15).

Animula (*p.* 65)

In this poem is the one full statement that Eliot has made of the nature of childhood. The world of the child, in the first part, has order and coherence, for each experience, whether in fact or fancy, is felt equally. Later the child loses this unity and finds only disorder, distrusting where previously it discriminated. Its soul becomes deadened, and it lives only after death. Hence, we must pray for these products of time, these souls that destroy themselves in various forms of violence.

1. This refers to Dante's *Purgatorio* (xviii. 86):

> From the hands of him who loves her before she is there issues like a simple child that plays, with weeping and laughter, the simple soul, that knows nothing except that, come from the hands of a glad creator, she turns willingly to everything that delights her. First she tastes the flavour of a trifling good; then is beguiled and pursues it, if neither guide nor check withhold her. Therefore laws were needed as a curb.

12. *running stags:* see l. 36.

19. Natural impulses conflict with moral necessity, free fantasy with actuality.

23. Encyclopædic information is its final retreat from life and reality.

31. *viaticum:* the last sacrament, given to persons in danger of death.

32, 33, 36. *Guitteriez, Boudin, Floret:* imaginary people, victims of the desire for knowledge or power or beauty.

36. Like Actaeon, who was turned into a stag (l. 12) and killed by his own hounds while in pursuit of Diana.

The Love Song of J. Alfred Prufrock (*p.* 67)

The hero with the important and yet slightly absurd name is a personification of the unsuccessful, the hesitant, the diffident, the futile, the self-pitying. His desire for love is also a desire for friendship and companionship and sympathy. The irony of calling the poem a "love song" lies in the fact that it will never be sung, and that Prufrock will never dare to voice his feelings. His life is trivial and insignificant, as are all his actions. His tragedy lies in the fact that he knows this and that he can see what would give his life meaning, but he lacks the courage and the initiative to change his way of life and his mediocre surroundings. He continues to postpone the decision. He is a man of intellect and humility who frankly confesses the triviality of his existence, and attempts, unsuccessfully, to decide the significance of his life and to take up a life with more meaning and depth. But, although he can see and analyse clearly his position, he cannot free himself from his old life or venture into a new life; polite resignation is his only solution, and he knows that is no solution.

The poem appears to be negative in its outlook, but it makes the positive assertion that Prufrock is a lost soul, to be pitied because of his sin of hesitation. Much of the setting of the poem is ugly and shadowy, a mediocre setting for a mediocre person, but beauty can be found in the pictures of what Prufrock might be.

The rhythm of the poem has the hesitancy of the character. The poem is leisurely and sometimes repeats itself, but the ultimate effect is one of concentration and economy. The imagery is drawn from any source. The language is colloquial and casual, but with mysterious and dark undertones and with occasional urgency. Out of the irony, the disconnectedness, the seeming digressions, the asides, the unpoetic language mixed with romantic and Shakespearean echoes, the relevant irrelevancies, is built up a whole, modern in tone, feeling, and expression.

> Our civilization comprehends great variety and complexity, and this variety and complexity, playing upon a refined sensibility, must produce various and complex results. The poet must become more and more comprehensive, more allusive, more indirect, in order to force, to dislocate if necessary, language into his meaning.
>
> T. S. ELIOT, Selected Essays

The Epigraph

"If I thought my answer were to one who ever could return to the world, this flame should shake no more; but since none ever did return alive from this depth, if what I hear be true, without fear of infamy I answer thee." This is the reply of the flame of Guido de Montefeltro in the penultimate circle of "that blind world" when he is asked by Dante to identify himself (Dante's *Inferno* XXVII. 61–6). One hopeless soul is speaking to another whom he believes to be hopeless also.

Guido and Prufrock are in similar situations of depression and hopelessness in the depths, and both make a confession of their plight and the cause of it in their own private hells.

1–3. The casual invitation, the intended activity, is opposed to an image of the desire for inactivity, even to the point of enforced release from pain. This remark of Prufrock's symbolizes his own problem: he is divided against himself, his mind is in conflict. The "you" is his other self.

4–9. The invitation is repeated. The romantic suggestions degenerate into the sordid and tedious cheapness of the town.

10–12. The streets suggest the character of the question, familiar and meaningless. A reason is given for the visit, but not the real reason.

13–14. His destination is a salon where the women talk of the sculptor of heroic figures, himself a hero. Their conversation, though on a difficult subject, is, ironically, self-assured and trivial. The jingle of the couplet suggests the superficiality of the conversation and, consequently, the commonplaceness of the society. The couplet serves as a refrain and suggests the endless routine of Prufrock's life.

15–22. Prufrock, unable to join in the conversation, turns to the window and the street. He indulges his imagination in images for the fog, which is itself a reflection of his own mental state in its inertia and solitariness.

23–34. There will be time for the fog to rouse itself from its inactivity; and there will be time for him—at first an escape, a postponement, then the closing of a trap as time shortens. The moment for the "overwhelming question" is tea-time.

29. A mock-heroic reference to Hesiod's *Works and Days*, the chief themes of which are the need for justice in a tyrannical age and the need for work. The poem is a kind of farmer's calendar. Hesiod, of the eighth century B.C., was the first Greek poet to seek his subject away from myth and fancy.

35–6. The place is again recalled in this haunting refrain.

37–48. The tension is increased by the question of daring being raised. The image of climbing stairs, with its suggestion of effort, stresses the difficulties of unromantic middle-age, as do the mock-heroic references to his "collar mounting firmly" and the "assertion" of his simple pin. But he dare not affirm his life courageously.

49–54. He is coming ever nearer to the room. He recalls all that his past life has been (l. 51): trivial, futile, full of meaningless social engagements in a dull routine. The change to the present tense of l. 52 indicates the imminence of the test; he is within sound of the room.

55–69. Three arguments are offered to prove that he should not "dare"—he knows the voices, arms, and eyes of the ladies, their organs of communication. But there has never been satisfactory communication between them and him: they are superior and disdainful, critical and supercilious. The "butt-ends" of l. 60 recall the kerbs and gutters of the city.

70–74. He begins, but he never finishes his proposal. His beginning about "lonely men" recalls the streets through which he came to the room. Then, he breaks out in an outburst of desperation and disgust at his own clumsiness and awkwardness compared with the self-confidence of the women. This sea imagery recurs at the end of the poem.

75–86. Tension decreases. The fog seems to have penetrated the salon. The rhyme of "ices" with "crises" is ironic, equating their importance. A number of heroic parallels, first suggested ironically in Michelangelo, is begun in an attempt at mock-heroic self-justification. The reference to John the Baptist (ll. 82–4) was anticipated by his preoccupation with his baldness (l. 40). He is no prophet, like John; his self-consciousness makes him prone to social discomfiture—shown in the image of his head "brought in upon a platter," as happened to John in the Bible and in Oscar Wilde's play, *Salome*. He has missed his great moment, and "the eternal Footman," who sees unerringly one's status and one's fate in society, has sniggered at his social defeat and inferiority.

87–98. Similarly, he might have been Lazarus, who returned from the dead (St John xi). If he tries to reveal his buried life, he will only meet with a rebuff, as did Lazarus, who found himself incapable of communicating his tremendous experience to his own society. Ll. 92–3 recall Marvell's poem, *To His Coy Mistress*, ll. 41–2:

> Let us roll all our strength and all
> Our sweetness up into one ball.

99–110. The magic lantern image puts his greatest fear, public revelation of his sensitivity, into its most vivid form.

111–119. He is also like Hamlet in that he procrastinates the fateful decision and he analyses his own character and the situation with clarity of mind. "To be" (in l. 111) is an echo of Hamlet's "To be or not to be, that is the question," but with a modern and ironic meaning: man was not "meant to be" but to become, to live and endure, to grow old, and to die. Prufrock then decides that, despite his indecision, he is not Hamlet, but rather the cautious attendant. He sees the truth of his character—careful, prudent, lacking initiative, playing a subordinate part. L. 118 recalls Chaucer's description of the Clerk of Oxford, "Ful of hy sentence" (packed with lofty wisdom)—*The Prologue*, l. 306.

120–25. Weariness is heard in the long, heavy sounds of l. 120. He decides to remain unromantic and to ponder over trivial matters such as whether he is to be a little sportive in dress. The mermaids, the sirens that sang to Odysseus, will not sing to him. Compare Donne's, "Teach me to hear mermaids singing."

126–31. The imagery of the sea, which began in l. 7 with "oyster-shells," returns, and the verse becomes lyrical. The sea is the image of his suppressed self, and reality returns with the last line which recalls "Talking of Michelangelo" and implies the rejection of the chance of self-realization and of redemption.

Mowing (*p.* 78)

1. Compare l. 14 of Edward Thomas's *The Manor Farm*.

10. *swale:* a hollow low place, a moist or marshy depression in a tract of land, especially in the midst of rolling prairie.

12. *orchises:* plants with rich, showy, often fragrant flowers.

After Apple-picking (*p.* 79)

This is a more intense and symbolic poem than is usual with Frost. The concrete experience of apple-picking is communicated firmly and realistically, but the task has a more universal application. The task of apple-picking is any task; it is life. The drowsiness afterwards may be the sleep of death, the end of the task bringing a feeling of completion and fulfilment.

40. *The woodchuck:* the North American marmot, a squirrel-like rodent about the size of a rabbit, which burrows in the ground and hibernates. The poet suggests by the reference to the woodchuck and its hibernation his own connexion with Nature and the cycle of the seasons.

Ghost House (*p.* 83)

16. *whippoorwill:* a species of goatsucker, a small North American nocturnal bird.

Two look at Two (*p.* 85)

6. *washout:* an erosion of earth by the action of water or the hole made by such.
15. *spruce:* a tree of the pine family.

Drummer Hodge (*p.* 93)

Hardy tells, in rhythm reminiscent of the ballads, of the pathetic incident of a young soldier who, killed probably in the Boer War, is buried on the veldt which means nothing to him, beneath stars whose names he does not know. The ironic and tragic implication is that he has fought, and died, for a cause that he did not understand; that he has been the plaything and the victim of a Fate, the "Immanent Will," that ignores the individual.

3. *kopje:* in South Africa, a small hill.

4. *veldt:* in South Africa, the name given to open, un-forested, or thinly-forested grass-country.

5. *foreign constellations:* such as the Southern Cross, a brilliant star group seen in the Southern hemisphere.

8. *Wessex:* used by Hardy to designate the South-west counties, especially Dorset.

9. *Karoo:* the name given to barren tracts in South Africa, consisting of extensive elevated plateaux, with a clayey soil, which during the dry season are entirely waterless and arid. Especially the Great Karoo and the Little Karoo to the East of Cape Town, between the coast and the veldt.

10. *Bush:* woodland; or uncleared or untilled districts, even those not wooded.

The Darkling Thrush (*p.* 93)

The note of hope at the end of the poem is the more telling because of the gloom of the time and the place and the bleakness of the description of the thrush itself as it sings ecstatically in a desolate and alien landscape.

5. *bine-stems:* the flexible shoots of a shrub or climbing plant, especially of the hop.

7. *haunted:* frequented. Note the ghostly associations of the word.

In Time of "The Breaking of Nations" (*p.* 95)

This poem, written in 1915 shortly after the outbreak of the First World War, refers in its title to Jeremiah LI. 20: "I will break in pieces the nations."

6. *ouch-grass:* a species of grass with long creeping root-stalks.

8. *Dynasties:* a succession of rulers of the same line or family.

Friends Beyond (*p.* 95)

The feeling of a village community for its past is vividly brought out in this poem. To them the past and the present are one, and one shades into the other. The poem deals with the actual and the real, the interests and activities of daily village life, in lines that linger over the past.

1. *William Dewy, Tranter Reuben:* two characters, father and son, in one of the earliest of Hardy's novels, *Under the Greenwood Tree*. A tranter is a carrier.

   Farmer Ledlow: a farmer of Mellstock, mentioned in *Under the Greenwood Tree*, Part I, Chapter IV.

3. *Mellstock:* the village in *Under the Greenwood Tree*. It is Stinsford, near Dorchester.

6. *leads:* leaded roofs.

9. *stillicide:* dripping of water from roofs of caves to form stalactites and stalagmites.

10. *bane:* that which causes ruin or woe.

16. *mid:* may.

    bass-viol: the precursor of the 'cello; a viol da gamba for playing the bass part in older concerted music.

17. *manse:* manor.

    hold in fee: own, have absolute and rightful possession of.

21. *quiz:* pry into and mock at.

    con: pore over.

22. *charlock:* a plant of the mustard family, with yellow flowers, which grows as a weed in cornfields.

23. *grinterns:* bins, compartments in granaries.

24. *blue china:* set of willow-pattern ware.

    ho: worry, grieve, be anxious.

29. *quire:* sing.

30. *stage:* stage-coach.

32. *Trine:* the Trinity, the Father, Son, and Holy Spirit as constituting one God.

33. *witteth:* knows.

The Choirmaster's Burial (*p.* 99)

13. *Mount Ephraim:* a hymn tune composed by Benjamin
    Milgrove (*c.* 1731–1810) and included in *Sixteen Hymns as
    they are sung at the Right Honourable the Countess of Hunting-
    don's Chapel in Bath* (1769). The psalm *Come all harmonious
    tongues*, by Isaac Watts, is sung to the tune of *Mount
    Ephraim* in *Cousin Phillis* (Part I) by Mrs Gaskell.
16. *seraphim:* Angels of the highest rank, celestial beings on
    either side of the Throne of God.

An August Midnight (*p.* 101)

4. *longlegs:* daddy-longlegs; the crane fly.
    dumbledore: usually, a humble or bumble bee; here,
    more probably, a cockchafer.

The Moth-signal (*p.* 101)

Egdon Heath is the heath-land between Dorchester and
Wareham. See Hardy's novel, *The Return of the Native*.
Hardy adapted the name from Eggardan (or -don), the
magnificent prehistoric hill fortress on the final chalk spur
of the Dorset headlands. See note on l. 4 of Andrew
Young's *A Prehistoric Camp*.

22. *tumulus:* an ancient burial mound.
32. *potsherds:* fragments of broken earthenware.
35. *thwartly:* adversely, unfortunately, unpropitiously.

Beyond the Last Lamp (*p.* 103)

A humble and humdrum event, a couple seen walking in
the rain, has given rise to a poem of universal applicability.
The sight of that couple still there after some hours has an
inexplicable pathos about it and to the poet has deep significance. The mysterious couple are more real than the
apparently real scene from which they have vanished.

Tooting Common is a two-hundred-acre common of grass, trees, and bushes in Wandsworth in South London.

The Voice (*p.* 105)

The desolation of the present is accepted in this poem as the natural accompaniment of human life. The sense of utter loss is not glossed over but accepted as inevitable. The ballad-like lilt of the opening soon changes to the matter-of-fact statement of l. 8 and the 'listlessness' of rhythm of l. 10. In the last stanza, with the hopelessness of the quest, the certainty of loneliness, comes a faltering in the rhythm, which finally breaks down in the last line, after a partial recovery in l. 15.

After a Journey (*p.* 106)

The poem is a retrospect in old age, when memory alone is active. The gulf of forty years is bridged, and for a moment the lonely present and the elusive past are one. But, however vivid the woman of forty years ago is, the present reasserts itself, and the gulf between is all the deeper and the more estranging for its temporary bridging. The slow and gentle rhythm preserves a balance between the present and the past.

At Castle Boterel (*p.* 107)

Beginning with details and particularities, the poem raises from these trivialities an image of the greatness and permanence of that moment, at one with the "primaeval rocks." The poem then returns to the particular moment, place, and person, and the poet's present desolation, which he accepts.

Castle Boterel is Boscastle in Cornwall, mentioned in *A Pair of Blue Eyes*.

During Wind and Rain (*p.* 108)

The poem is an elegy, mourning those who used to live in the house and now inhabit "a high new house"—the house of death. With the simplest of domestic detail a picture is built up of a household ordinary in its homeliness but yet universal in its significance, as is the loss. Each stanza has a season as background, beginning with winter in the first; it is implied that the moving house takes place in autumn, for so many things the season of change.

5. *mooning:* the word makes the picture of the faces indistinct.

6. This refrain is as if from some half-remembered song. It recalls us from the past we are lingering over to the desolate present.

7. The last line of each stanza gives a wider background, symbolic of transience and death, to the picture of present grief. It sets it against the background of eternal Nature and ineluctable Fate.

28. *ploughs:* It is important that the last metaphor is from farming and hence suggests inevitability as well as continuity.

The Confirmation (*p.* 115)

The poem expresses the transfiguration, by love, of the two lovers.

Horses (*p.* 115)

The horses of his father's farm in the bare Orkneys appear to the poet as symbols of wonder and terror. Beauty comes from his recollections of early childhood, but at the same time he remembers what he has lost. Compare Wordsworth's *Ode on Intimations of Immortality* and Coleridge's

Ode to Dejection, where the two poets regret that they are no longer able to see the visions of childhood: "There hath passed away a glory from the earth." (For a modern prose counterpart, see Herbert Read's *The Innocent Eye*, memories of his childhood.) Compare the later poem, *The Horses*.

11. *seraphim:* Angels of the highest rank, celestial beings on either side of the Throne of God.

15. *bossy:* rounded.

18. *gloam:* gloaming, twilight.

22. *apocalyptic:* of the nature of a revelation.

The Difficult Land (*p.* 116)

The poet may be referring to the Orkneys, in which he spent his childhood, or, more probably, to Scotland. He paints the picture of a nation without hope, yet brave and enduring. He finds nobility in their perseverance through defeat and privation and frustration.

The Child Dying (*p.* 118)

7–8. These two lines might belong to a sentimental children's hymn; but the effect is not sentimental or, as it would be in an early Eliot poem, ironical. The words are used at their face value.

13–18. The images chosen to indicate memory are commonplace, but they convey precisely the simple things to which memory clings.

The Horses (*p.* 120)

Compare the earlier poem, *Horses*. The horses of his father's farm reappear here as harbingers of a new simplicity, of the lost communion with nature, of the release of natural emotion.

45–52. Man has met and survived disaster. These animals,

who have never known the Fall and the loss of Eden, are willing to co-operate with man and share his world of guilt and remorse.

Into thirty centuries born (*p.* 122)

12. *Ilium:* the inner citadel of Troy, burnt by the Greeks when Troy was captured and destroyed.
16. *the rout:* the crowd of ordinary citizens.
18. *Priam:* the king of Troy. In his young days he was a mighty warrior; but at the outbreak of the Trojan War he was so old and feeble that he took no part in the combat. He met his death in the sack of the city. See *Hamlet* II. 2. 481–549.
26. *Methuselah:* proverbial for the long life attributed to him in Genesis v. 27.
30. the Garden of Eden.
39. an echo of *Macbeth* v. 5. 18–19:

> To-morrow, and to-morrow, and to-morrow,
> Creeps in this petty pace from day to day.

The Manor Farm (*p.* 127)

4. The homely and pithy humour of a countryman, with a touch of folk-lore about it.
14. A close verbal echo of l. 1 of Frost's *Mowing*: "There was never a sound beside the wood but one."

Swedes (*p.* 128)

The poet has seen a common sight with that vividness of detail that is a sign of love.
6. *the Valley of the Tombs of Kings:* at Thebes, city of ancient Egypt, situated on both sides of the Nile. The village of Luxor now stands on the site. There are many temples of gods and tombs of kings there.

7. *a Pharaoh's tomb:* Pharaoh is the generic name of the ancient Egyptian kings.

11. *Amen-hotep:* Amen-hotep III, Egyptian king, reigned 1411-1375 B.C. A successful warrior and a great builder. He consolidated the empire. He raised along the banks of the Nile monuments unsurpassed for their grandeur and the perfection of their workmanship.

Tall Nettles (*p.* 128)

Colloquial in phrasing and rhythm, the poem begins meditatively, quietly, almost diffidently, to flower into the last two epigrammatic lines, which make a discovery with an air of authority. The poet is being wholly sincere when he says he loves derelict corners of farmyards and the dust on nettles: such things fulfilled a need in him.

The Glory (*p.* 130)

A description of the morning's beauty leads to a meditation on the nature of beauty and of happiness. He does not know the answers to the questions he asks, and he makes the poem out of his not knowing the answers. He hardly even knows what he is looking for. The poet has the courage of his lack of conviction.

20. The irony of this line lies in the diffident "perhaps."

October (*p.* 131)

The poem reproduces at the beginning (ll. 1-8) the details of an October day as described in his prose work *Wales*; but what is in prose a description of a scene becomes in the poem the presentment of a mood, and the poem ends with a glimpse of the poet's inner life.

4. *scabious:* a herbaceous plant, formerly believed to be efficacious for the cure of certain skin diseases.

tormentil: a long-growing rosaceous herb, with four-petalled yellow flowers, of trailing habit, common on heaths and dry pastures; in use from early times for medicine and tanning. Sometimes called septfoil.

8. *gossamers:* the fine filmy substance consisting of cobwebs spun by small spiders, which seem floating in the air, especially in autumn, or spread over a grassy surface.

There appears to be a stress omitted in this line, but, if we accent the last syllable of "gossamers," we get a kind of airy sustaining of the word and a movement in the whole line which suggests the light, erratic, wayward flight of the gossamers.

Home (*p.* 131)

Even in the countryside he so much loved, Thomas was never entirely quite at home. Part of him was chafing to be off—somewhere. As this poem suggests, he was chafing at the limitations of life itself: it was this chafing that prevented him from putting down his roots permanently in any one place.

Roads (*p.* 132)

33. *Helen:* daughter of a British chief, wife of the Emperor Maximus, A.D. 383–8. She made high roads, Roman roads. Also, the poet's wife, Helen Thomas. For the story of their courtship and marriage see Helen Thomas's *As It Was* (1926) and *World without End* (1931).

35. *the Mabinogion tales:* a collection of Welsh tales of the fourteenth and fifteenth centuries. They deal with old Celtic legends and mythology, in which the supernatural and magical play the chief part. Lady Charlotte Guest published a translation of them, 1838–49.

53. *to France:* to the trenches and the War, the First World War against Germany, 1914–18.

Old Man (*p.* 135)

Here Thomas is dealing, at first, with something we all know—how a smell can bring a memory or a feeling that there is a memory connected with it. Beginning with a quiet meditation upon the plant, the poem passes to the child, thence to the poignant realization of death. Instead of describing the flower in terms of his own childhood, Thomas gives a picture of his little daughter, thus giving the thoughts and feelings aroused by the flower a more general truth—it is every child that gathers the flower and so gains a little more of experience, to be remembered one day perhaps or to be lost beyond recall, but still leaving a mark on the mind. The poem ends on a note of mystery, of the ultimate mystery of life and death and eternity. The poem has the quiet tone, the familiar diction and the speech rhythms that Thomas used so characteristically to record his experiences. The groping, hesitating manner well suits the attempt to capture an elusive memory.

1. *Old Man, or Lad's-love:* the plant is southernwood, a hardy deciduous shrub having a fragrant aromatic smell and a sour taste. It was formerly much cultivated for medicinal purposes. The contrast and the paradox of the two names in the title are significant of the two ways of seeing things of everyday life, and also subtly suggest the passage of time, as do the references to the child and the grown-up, to the "ancient damson trees," and to "the hoar-green feathery herb, almost a tree" and the "hoar-green bush." Age is trying to recall something out of its youth.

4. *rosemary:* for remembrance. Compare *Hamlet* iv. 5. 174: "There's rosemary, that's for remembrance."

9–10. The deep contrast between liking and loving.

20–21. Again contrast, between "that bitter scent" and "damson trees."

29–31. The meaning of the poem—the difference between liking and loving. It carries conviction because it has grown out of the experience.

34–35. These two lines admirably describe Thomas's characteristic manner.

36. The man-made path (the "bent path to a door" of l. 22) is contrasted with the mysterious and other-worldly "avenue dark, nameless, without end" of l. 39.

Words (*p.* 136)

20. *the burnet rose:* the Scottish wild rose.

48–49. *Whose nightingales have no wings:* the sweetest singers in Wales are the men and women.

Lights Out (*p.* 138)

The personal note is strong in this poem: his delight in love, books, and the "face of dearest look." The sleep he longs for, the death of consciousness, is also death itself—at the end of the long day, when "Lights out" is sounded on the bugles. The poem "goes into the unknown" of himself further than any other.

11. *now blurs:* the two consecutive stresses produce a clogging effect. The travellers are slowed up, bogged down; they can get no farther. This anticipates the next line.

13. *Here love ends:* these three consecutive stresses drive home this sense of finality. The sleep is the sleep of death.

The Other (*p.* 140)

This poem deals with the poet's quest for his "other" self, his real self, his deepest self. This search for the ultimate reality about himself goes on against the mysterious, quiet, and lonely background of the forest and the noisy interchange of inn and village. The diction and the rhythm are the familiar ones of speech. Now and again in its ideas and phrasing and rhythm the poem recalls George Herbert's *Pilgrimage*, with lines like "A long it was and weary way," and "A wasted place but sometimes rich." The mysterious atmosphere of the poem is enhanced by the fact that at one point the pursuer becomes the pursued and at another he admits that he does not know the purpose of the pursuit or what he will do if it succeeds; the underlying suggestion is that the search will never succeed in this life. The poem begins with "the forest," a frequent symbol in Thomas's poetry. It is the dark and pathless region of human experience, which thought or reason cannot explore, only the subconscious or the imagination; it is eternity lying in wait behind the temporal; or it is simply sleep, or death. The inns and the roads are a refuge from it.

67. *crocketed*: as if decorated with crockets, small ornaments placed on the inclined sides of pinnacles, etc.; usually in the form of buds or curled leaves.

Out in the dark (*p.* 143)

The dark is more than physical dark. Thomas does not anticipate immortality. The short lines have a delicate and subtle movement.

An Irish Airman foresees his Death (*p.* 148)

The airman was Robert Gregory, who was killed in Italy in 1918. The repetition in the poem is subtle and has something of the charm of an incantation.

3–4. The attitude is both heroic and bitter, arrogant and self-dramatizing.

5. *Kiltartan*: in County Galway.

Easter 1916 (*p.* 148)

The Dublin Rebellion of Easter 1916 is believed, in spite of its immediate failure, to have been the beginning of modern Ireland. Yeats was in Dublin when it happened, and, though at first he deplored the bloodshed and thought the sacrifice of its leaders wasteful, he soon came to see the unselfishness of the sacrifice, which made a deep impression on the Irish people. Yeats deliberately included in the company of heroes one who had done Yeats's friends "most bitter wrong"—"he, too, has been changed." His emotions concerning the event are mixed and they are all in the poem —wonder, exaltation, pity, forgiveness, hope, resignation. From the doubt that those who act like this may find their hearts turned to stone by sacrificing themselves for a cause, an abstraction, he passes to the hope that good may follow.

17. *That woman:* probably Maud Gonne, the "loveliest woman" in Ireland. She had been brought up in the atmosphere of the Viceregal court, her father being an officer in the British garrison in Dublin, but the sight of the eviction of poverty-stricken Irish tenants by absentee English landlords had roused in her an intense feeling of nationalism. She dreamt of becoming an Irish Joan of Arc. She inspired Yeats's early love-poetry (she was "Helen of Troy" to him) and he dedicated his play, *The Countess Cathleen,* to her. He proposed to her in 1899, but was rejected. She married John M. MacBride in 1902, but they were separated in 1905. MacBride was executed with fifteen others after the 1916 Easter Rising. Maud Gonne, a political prisoner in England, escaped to Dublin in 1918.

31. *This other man:* probably MacBride.

43. *Enchanted to a stone:* the stone symbolizes what is eternal and monumental in their death.

58. *Can make a stone of the heart:* can make a heart lose all human feeling and sensibility. The dual symbolism of the "stone" suggests the conflict in Yeats's mind between the two views of the cause—whether it justifies the sacrifice of living persons to it, or whether it kills all personal feelings in the heart.

75. *MacDonagh:* Irish Socialist leader. Executed after the Rising.

    MacBride: see note on l. 17.

76. *Connolly:* James Connolly, 1870–1916. Irish Socialist. Commander-in-Chief of the Easter Week Rising. Executed on May 12.

    Pearse: Patrick Henry Pearse, 1879–1916. Irish educator, writer, and patriot; a leader in the Easter Rising. Designated President of Ireland's provisional government. Read the proclamation of the Irish Republic on Easter Monday. For six days they held out in the General Post Office and other main buildings in Dublin, but surrendered on Saturday, April 20. On May 3 he was executed.

The Second Coming (*p.* 151)

Yeats has a vision, a moment of insight into the future. It arises from a mood of doubt and despair, inspired by the anarchy of the world, the increase of bloodshed, and the growth of disbelief. He sees the present era as dying; the first two thousand years of Christianity have brought discord and strife because man has forgotten Christ. The new era that is about to be born is symbolized by the "rough beast," which is the antithesis of the gentle Bethlehem. It is not sought for or created: it comes uninvited, unwanted almost, upon the consciousness. This helps to give the poem the force of objectivity. It is Yeats's theory that a period of anarchy and violence follows a period of innocence and beauty.

1. *gyre:* see note on *Sailing to Byzantium,* l. 19.

2. *The falcon:* man who has lost touch with Christianity ("the falconer" is Christ). The image is derived from Dante.

12. *Spiritus Mundi:* this term is Yeats's own adaptation of a term coined by the seventeenth-century Platonist,

Henry More, in whose works Yeats was deeply versed. More's own term was *anima mundi*—he thinks of an animating spirit. Yeats thinks rather of a spiritual repository, a racial memory of basic human experience (*mundi*), what Jung called the "racial, or collective, unconscious."

14. *a shape*: like a sphinx, and symbolizing both evil and wisdom.

17. *indignant desert birds*: vultures, ominous and destructive. Compare:

> Call on your father now before your bones
> Have been picked bare by the great desert birds.
>
> *Calvary*

21. *rough beast*: perhaps an echo of the beasts of Revelation (XIII), which bring destruction.

Coole Park and Ballylee, 1931 (*p. 152*)

At Coole, a country house near Galway, lived Lady Gregory, a woman of genius. All men of talent, all profound men, gathered there. This poem was written shortly before her death.

W. B. YEATS

Lady Gregory helped to found, and wrote plays for, the Abbey Theatre, Dublin. She had sold Coole to the Land Commission and the Department of Forestry in 1927. In 1929 Yeats had prophesied its coming ruin in *The Wild Swans at Coole*. Now Yeats feels the passing of its glory. Lady Gregory is dying and he remembers their past work. His prophecy was fulfilled: the Forestry Department sold the house and it was pulled down.

4. *'dark' Raftery's 'cellar'*: "The blind poet Raftery called the great hole where the river sank underground 'The Cellar.'"—W. B. YEATS.

8. *water*: "The poem is intricate with metaphor. The swan and water are emblems of the soul and inspiration."—W. B. YEATS.

12. *tragic buskin:* the high thick-soled boot (*cothurnus*) worn in Athenian tragedy.

14. *swan:* see note on l. 8.

47. *Homer:* the poet to whom is assigned by very ancient tradition the authorship of the two epic poems, the *Iliad* and the *Odyssey*.

A Prayer for my Daughter (*p.* 154)

In this poem are prominent Yeats's aversion to coarseness and vulgarity, his romantic regret for the past, and his desire for an aristocratic civilization.

4. *Gregory's wood:* see note on Lady Gregory in *Coole Park and Ballylee,* 1931.

25. *Helen:* Helen of Troy, the divinely beautiful daughter of Zeus and Leda. In the absence of her husband, Menelaus, she was carried away to Troy by Paris, the son of Priam. This was the origin of the Trojan War.

26. *a fool:* Paris.

27. *that great Queen:* Venus, who was born rising from the sea.

29. *smith:* Venus's husband, Hephaestus (Vulcan).

59. *the loveliest woman born:* Maud Gonne. See note on *Easter 1916,* l. 17.

73-74. Yeats's aristocratic ideal.

Sailing to Byzantium (*p.* 157)

Byzantium was a Greek city built on the eastern part of the site of Constantinople, in which it was merged in A.D. 330. At the division of the Eastern and Western Empires between his two sons on the death of Theodosius in 395, Byzantium became the capital of the Eastern Empire till 1453. Its situation was remarkable for its beauty and security. The church of Santa Sophia embodies the surviving monuments.

In the poem, Byzantium is a holy city, because it is the

capital of Eastern Christendom and because it is Yeats's holy city and heaven of imagination. It has inherited the perfection of craftsmanship.

> In the fifth century . . . Byzantium became Byzantine, and substituted for formal Roman magnificence, with its glorification of physical power, an architecture that suggests the sacred City in the Apocalypse of St John. I think if I could be given a month of Antiquity and leave to spend it where I chose, I would spend it in Byzantium a little before Justinian opened St Sophia and closed the Academy of Plato. I think I could find in some little wine-shop some philosophical worker in mosaic who could answer all my questions, the supernatural descending near to him . . . for the pride of his delicate skill would make what was an instrument of power to princes and clerics and a murderous madness in the mob, show as a lovely flexible presence like that of a perfect human body.
>
> I think that in early Byzantium, maybe never before or since in recorded history, religious, aesthetic and practical life were one, that architect and artificers . . . spoke to the multitude and the few alike. The painter, the mosaic worker, the worker in gold and silver, the illuminator of sacred books, were almost impersonal, almost perhaps without the consciousness of individual design, absorbed in their subject-matter and that the vision of a whole people.
>
> W. B. YEATS, *A Vision*, 279–80[1]

Byzantium had been a province of the Roman Empire, under which authority it had suffered from unimaginative treatment of its own ancient traditions. Yeats saw a parallel between Rome and England as imperialistic powers, and imagined Ireland as a new Byzantium breaking loose from its masters so that it might develop its own culture and art, philosophy and religion.

The poem is an attempt to praise eternity as a means of forgetting regrets for past youth and vigour. The poet's

[1] *By kind permission of Messrs Macmillan and Co., Ltd, and Mrs W. B. Yeats.*

country is a land of natural beauty, beauty of body. But his own body is old; therefore, the soul must sing the more loudly to compensate for the dying flesh. But the only way whereby the soul can learn to sing is by studying works of the soul. Therefore, he has sailed to Byzantium, for the artists there do not follow the forms of nature but intellectual forms of ideal patterns. He implores them to sever him from his dying body and to gather him into an "artifice of eternity."

The poem can be taken on at least four levels: as the transition from sensual art to intellectual art; as the poet's insight into the nature of Byzantine imagination; as the poet's coming to terms with age and death; and as the poet's conception of Ireland and its destiny in art.

1–8. These lines express great regret and nostalgia at leaving the country of the young and of physical love with their strength and vitality.

2. *birds in the trees:* this ironic reference to Keats's *Ode to a Nightingale* adds to the tension.

4. *the salmon-falls:* a visual memory of Sligo River which drops through the town in a series of shallow falls up which the fish leap on their way to Lough Gill. This suggests spring-time and the strength and grace of the leaping salmon.

the mackerel-crowded seas: the appearance of shoals of mackerel out in the bay excites the fishing village to put to sea with the prospect of a rich harvest in the nets.

5. *commend:* the word is the key-word and carries the stress. It is emphasized by the colloquial "fish, flesh, or fowl," which "commend" their life-cycle and their death. Compare:

> All that could run or leap or swim
> Whether in wood, water or cloud,
> Acclaiming, proclaiming, declaiming Him.
>
> *The Dancer at Cruachan and Cro-Patrick*

7. *caught:* again the key-word, as its place of emphasis in the line suggests. Man is "caught" as in a net.

8. For an old man there is nothing left but the great achievements of the past. Self-irony is in this line, as in l. 10.

9–16. The theme of this stanza, and indeed of the whole poem, is found in this letter of William Blake's:

> I have been very near the gates of death, and have returned very weak, and an old man feeble and tottering, but not in spirits and life, not in the real man, the imagination which liveth forever. In that I am stronger and stronger as this foolish body decays.

10. Compare "There is a comfortable kind of old scare-crow" and "Old clothes upon old sticks to scare a bird," in *Among School Children*.

11. Derived from Blake's vision of his brother's soul flying up to heaven and clapping its hands for joy.

17. *God's holy fire:* a reference to Isaiah's live coal with which one of the seraphim touched his lips (Isaiah VI. 67); and to the theories of Plotinus (born *c.* A.D. 205), the essence of whose philosophy was the desire to escape from the body and from the material world. The image is also related to Plate 84 in Blake's illustrations for Dante—"Dante entering the Holy Fire."

18. Yeats had first seen this Byzantine mosaic at Ravenna in 1907, where a great frieze on the walls of St Apollinare Nuovo shows martyrs in a fire.

19. *perne in a gyre:* the perne is the spool or bobbin on which thread is spun. The image here is that of a shuttle revolving round and up the walls of the course of time, leaving behind it the thread as a clue by which the depths may be explored again. (Compare *Byzantium*, ll. 11–12.) The gyre is the conical spiral of determined events in which man and events move. Compare:

> Though I had long perned in the gyre,
> Between my hatred and desire

and

> To watch a white gull take
> A bit of bread thrown up into the air;
> Now gyring down and perning there
>
> *Demon and Beast*

24. Compare, "That supreme art which is to win us from life and gather us into eternity like doves into their dove-cotes."—*The Tables of the Law.*

25–32. The ghost can return, and take what shape its imagination allows: but nothing less than the perfection of the artificers will suffice. Yeats wishes to be the singing voice of eternity fashioned by the eternal artificers.

27–32. "I have read somewhere that in the Emperor's palace at Byzantium was a tree made of gold and silver, and artificial birds that sang."—W. B. YEATS. Compare Marlowe's *Hero and Leander*, 1. 31–2:

> Where sparrows perched, of hollow pearl and gold,
> Such as the world would wonder to behold.

Byzantium (*p.* 158)

Like *Sailing to Byzantium*, this poem is an attempt to praise the eternity of art as a means of forgetting regrets for youth and vigour; but this poem is also a description of the act of making a poem from a number of images.

The poem falls into five parts: the background of the city with its violent contrasts; the invocation of death and the wisdom of past ages; the goldsmith's art which is permanent; the mosaics (see note on *Sailing to Byzantium*, l. 18), which give the permanence of art to the spiritual experience; the spirits, made triumphant and permanent by the artist, triumph over the body, "mire and blood."

1. *images:* the reflected shades of reality.

2. That the soldiers of the great Emperor are drunk is the ironic paradox of empire. The homely colloquial "abed" jars, deliberately, with its false rhyme to "recede."

5. *dome:* the symbol of Byzantine achievement and of Heaven. It does not scorn man but how he simplifies his complexities. The image is an echo of Shelley's *Adonais:*

> Life, like a dome of many-coloured glass,
> Stains the white radiance of Eternity.

8. *fury:* compare the Psalms: "My fury it upheld me." Here, the poet's creative urge.

9–16. The dead are invoked to discover their wisdom.

9. *image:* the shade in a materialized condition.
    shade: disembodied spirit.

11–12. See note on *Sailing to Byzantium,* l. 19. It also suggests the legend of Theseus' killing of the Minotaur in the labyrinth, and of Orpheus and Eurydice.

14. *breathless:* without breath (*i.e.,* dead), and also out of breath with excitement, haste, or exhaustion.

16. Compare Coleridge's *The Ancient Mariner:*

> The Nightmare Life-in-Death was she,
> Who thicks man's blood with cold.

17–24. See the note on *Sailing to Byzantium,* ll. 27–32, and l. 30 of the poem.

19. *star-lit:* compare l. 5. The constancy of the star-light is contrasted with the inconstancy of the moon.
    golden bough: a reference to Sir John Fraser's monumental work on antiquity and its legends, *The Golden Bough.*

20. The bird belongs both to the world of the dead and to the world of immortality; it is a sentinel to the underworld and to the earth. It is above all change.

21. *embittered:* scorned.

23. *common bird:* the ordinary bird that is mortal and temporary.

25–32. The mosaics on the Emperor's pavement. Yeats had read *The Age of Justinian and Theodora*, by W. G. Holmes, in which is described the Forum of Constantine, known as 'The Pavements.'

26. *Flames . . . faggot:* these suggest martyrdom or the devastation of a country by soldiers.

   steel: flint, and a sword.

33. The dolphin is the escort of the dead to Paradise, and also the rescuer of humanity from the complexities of mire and blood. Arion, who won the music prize in Sicily (Yeats had won the Nobel Prize for Literature in 1923), had been flung overboard with his lyre by the seamen of his ship and had been rescued by a dolphin. Compare *Twelfth Night* I. 2. 15: "Like Arion on a dolphin's back."

34. *The smithies break the flood:* the flood symbolizes the confusion, the complexity. The art of Byzantium, of the workers in gold who hammer out the metal, is suggested by "break" in one of its meanings; the other meaning suggests the contrast, the opposition, of fire and water.

35. *golden:* because of the metal or because of the Emperor's power and value.

36–37. The mosaics with their formal patterns impose order on complexity, the order of proportion. The "marbles" suggest coldness and perpetuity as well as pattern, the pattern or rhythm of the dance.

37. *furies:* compare l. 8. With "flood" in l. 33, "furies" again suggests fire and water, the two aspects of life reconciled by art.

40. *gong-tormented:* see l. 4. Compare:

> All men are dancers and their tread
> Goes to the barbarous clangour of a gong.

Nineteen Hundred and Nineteen

An Acre of Grass (*p.* 159)

Yeats feels that he does not share the interests of his contemporaries. He can give to the world only his poetry, and he has no ambition to discover anything new. But what he cannot obtain through flashes of inspiration or hard work, he will obtain through intensity of feeling and profundity of thought.

7–12. Neither imagination nor the rags and bones of old memory can make truth known.

13–24. Frenzy can create truth. Truth, as represented by the frenzy of an old man, means a position with the great frenzied minds of the past.

15. *Timon:* an Athenian of the fifth century B.C., who, owing to the ingratitude of his friends, became a misanthrope. He later discovered a buried treasure, and when his friends, attracted by this, sought him once more, he drove them away with contumely. Shakespeare's *Timon of Athens* is based on the story.

Lear: Shakespeare's King Lear.

16. *William Blake:* poet, painter, and mystic (1757–1827). Yeats was devoted to the image of Blake and what Blake stands for. In Blake Yeats found authority for the glorification of the imagination rather than the world of action. Blake combined qualities that belong both to the man of action and to the dreamer.

19. *Michael Angelo:* Buonarroti, great Italian sculptor, painter and poet (1475–1564). The ceiling of the Sistine Chapel at Rome was painted 1508–12; the great fresco of the Last Judgment 1535–41 (l. 22).

The Stockdoves (*p.* 163)

Stockdoves are wild pigeons.

7. *Ballard Down:* in Dorset.

The Dead Crab (*p.* 164)

5. *cote-armure:* coat of mail.

The Lane (*p.* 166)

6. *guelder:* the guelder-rose, named from Guelders (in Prussia) or Guelderland (a province of Holland); the snow-ball tree, with globular clusters of white flowers.

wayfaring-tree: a tall, white-flowered shrub growing wild in hedges and underwood.

Late Autumn (*p.* 168)

2. *share:* the iron blade of a plough which cuts the ground.
3. *rape:* a plant closely allied to the turnip, cultivated for its herbage and oil-producing seeds.
4. *charlock:* a plant of the mustard family, with yellow flowers, which grows as a weed in cornfields.

Last Snow (*p.* 169)

4. *ride:* a road or way for riding on horseback, especially through a wood.
6. *spathe:* outer sheath protecting certain plants as they appear through the earth.
10. *spear:* the leaf or shoot of a snowdrop.

A Prehistoric Camp (*p.* 170)

4. *Eggardon:* a hamlet and hill in South-west Dorset, five miles North-east of Bridport. The hill is crowned by an Iron-Age, pre-Roman, hill fort. See note on Hardy's *The Moth Signal.*
11. *earthworks:* banks or mounds of earth used as a rampart or fortification.

Wiltshire Downs (*p.* 170)

Wiltshire is a county of South-west England, containing many ancient monuments, including Stonehenge. The Downs are the treeless undulating chalk uplands of South England, serving chiefly for pasturage.

4. *pipit:* a bird of a family with a general resemblance to larks.

    stare: starling.

6. *divots:* slices of earth with the grass growing on them—turfs, sods.

9. *windhover:* a name for the kestrel, from its habit of hovering in the air with its head to the wind. A kestrel is a small falcon or hawk.

12. *shearlings:* sheep that have been shorn once.

    tegs: sheep in their second year, or from the time they are weaned till their first shearing—yearling sheep.

    yoes: ewes, female sheep.

13. *barrow:* a mound raised over graves in prehistoric times.

14. *farrow:* litter.

The Roman Wall (*p.* 171)

3. *the ancient wall:* Hadrian's Wall. Built by the Roman Emperor Hadrian about A.D. 121. It extended from the Tyne to the Solway Firth, from Wallsend to Bowness, about seventy-three miles. It is a continuous rampart with a ditch in front of it, a number of small forts along it, and one or two outposts a few miles to the North of it. It marked the definite limit of the Roman world.

4. *whitlow-grass:* a small British saxifrage, formerly reputed to cure whitlows, sores, or swellings in fingers or thumbs.

    pranks: adorns, spangles, decks gaily and brightly.

9. *cist:* a sepulchral chest consisting of a stone-covered

coffin formed of slabs placed on edge and covered on the
top by one or more horizontal slabs.

12. *fells:* moorland ridges.

14. *scallops:* shell-fish.

18. *sough:* sighing.

20. *Crag Lough:* four miles north-east of Haltwhistle, in
Northumberland. The lake nestles at the base of the
cliffs two hundred feet high, on which is perched the Wall.

Additional Note to "An Irish Airman foresees his Death" (*p.* 148).

Mr A. P. Rossiter[1] writes:

The airman dismisses hatred, public service, subserv-
ience to law, the applause of crowds, with the contempt of a
man accustomed to think for himself and feel for himself
privately, irrespective of what *public* voices may say. The
airman is also a poetic symbol representing the difference
between the personal, unmistakable, deeper emotions and
the shallower sentiments of the crowd. . . . With the same
lucid clarity of vision that he brings to bear on himself,
the airman rejects a false patriotism and insists the more
firmly on the true. He loves his village; he loves with
virile hardness the excitement of aerial combat; but the
two feelings have no direct connexion with one another. . . .
The peculiar position of an Irish fighter in 1914–18 has
provided the poet with 'an image': a symbol representative
of the poet's sharp discrimination between feelings that
may be called 'sincere' and those we must, by contrast, call
'factitious.' The 'lonely impulse' is, as it were, a *sample* of
genuine experience.

[1] *This Living Language,* by A. P. Rossiter, by kind permission
of Messrs Longmans, Green and Co. Ltd.

INDEX OF FIRST LINES

READING LIST

THE editor has found helpful the following books of criticism, and he expects that the teacher and the pupil will also find them of use:

BROOKS, CLEANTH, *Modern Poetry and the Tradition* (Auden, Frost, Yeats); P. L. Poetry, London (1948).

BOWRA, C. M., *The Heritage of Symbolism* (Yeats); Macmillan (1943).

SAVAGE, D. S., *The Personal Principle* (Auden, Eliot, Yeats); Routledge (1944).

WILSON, EDMUND, *Axel's Castle* (Eliot, Yeats); Scribner's Sons (1947).

MURRY, J. MIDDLETON, *Aspects of Literature* (Hardy, Thomas); Cape (1920).

SPENDER, STEPHEN, *Poetry since 1939*; Longmans (1946).

ISAACS, J., *The Background of Modern Poetry*; Bell (1951).

WILLIAMS, CHARLES, *Poetry at Present*; Oxford (1930).

TSCHUMI, R., *Thought in Twentieth-century English Poetry* (Auden, Eliot, Muir, Yeats); Routledge (1957)

BOWRA, C. M., *Inspiration and Poetry* (Hardy); Macmillan (1955).

HUXLEY, ALDOUS, *On the Margin* (Thomas); Chatto (1923).

MACNEICE, LOUIS, *Modern Poetry*; Oxford (1938).

LEAVIS, F. R., *New Bearings in English Poetry*; Chatto (1932).

SPENDER, STEPHEN, *The Creative Element* (Auden, Eliot, Yeats); Hamish Hamilton (1953).

KNIGHTS, L. G., *Explorations* (Yeats); Chatto (1946).

BULLOUGH, G., *The Trend of Modern Poetry*; Routledge (1938).

MUIR, EDWIN, *The Present Age from 1914*; Cresset (1938).

PALMER, HERBERT, *Post-Victorian Poetry*; Dent (1938).

TILLYARD, E. M. W., *Poetry Direct and Oblique*; Chatto (1945).

POWELL, DILYS, *Descent from Parnassus*; Cresset (1935).

BRONOWSKI, J., *A Poet's Defence*; Faber (1940).

BOWRA, C. M., *The Background of Modern Poetry*; Oxford (1944).

DEUTSCH, B., *This Modern Poetry*; Faber (1937).

BAILEY, RUTH, *A Dialogue on Modern Poetry*; Oxford (1938).

HOGGART, RICHARD, *Auden*; Chatto (1951).

SCARFE, FRANCIS, *Auden and After*; Routledge (1940).

LEHMANN, JOHN, *The Whispering Gallery* (Auden); Longmans (1955).

DUFFIN, H. C., *Walter de la Mare*; Sidgwick and Jackson (1949).

REID, FORREST, *Walter de la Mare*; Secker (1915).

PRESTON, RAYMOND, "*Four Quartets" Rehearsed*; Sheed and Ward (1948).

RAJAN, EDWARD B., *T. S. Eliot. A Study of his Writings by Several Hands*; Dennis Dobson (1947).

WAIN, JOHN, *Interpretations (Prufrock)*; Routledge (1955).

GARDNER, HELEN, *The Art of T. S. Eliot*; Cresset (1949).

MAXWELL, D. E. S., *The Poetry of T. S. Eliot*; Routledge (1952).

MATTHIESSEN, F. O., *The Achievement of T. S. Eliot*; Oxford (1947).

WILLIAMSON, G., *A Reader's Guide to T. S. Eliot*; Thames and Hudson (1955).

BROWN, DOUGLAS, *Thomas Hardy*; Longmans (1954).

JOHNSON, LIONEL, *The Art of Thomas Hardy*; Methuen (1891).

RICHARDS, I. A., *Science and Poetry* (Hardy); Routledge (1926).

HALL, JOHN, *Edwin Muir*; Longmans (1956).

COOMBES, H., *Edward Thomas*; Chatto (1956).

LEWIS, C. DAY, *The Poetry of Edward Thomas* (Essays by Divers Hands, Vol. 28, Royal Society of Literature); Oxford (1956).

HENN, T. R., *The Lonely Tower—Studies in the Poetry of Yeats*; Methuen (1950).

JEFFARES, A. NORMAN, *W. B. Yeats, Man and Poet*; Routledge (1949).

ELLMANN, RICHARD, *Yeats: The Man and the Masks*; Macmillan (1949).

RUDD, MARGARET, *Divided Image—A Study of Blake and Yeats*; Routledge (1953).

MACNEICE, LOUIS, *The Poetry of W. B. Yeats*; Oxford (1941).

ROSSITER, A. P., *Our Living Language* (Yeats); Longmans (1953).

HOWARTH, HERBERT, *The Irish Writers* 1880–1940; Rockcliff (1958).

THWAITE, ANTHONY, *Contemporary English Poetry*; Heinemann (1959).

CLARK, LEONARD (Editor), *Andrew Young—Prospect of a Poet*; Hart-Davis (1957).